THE THWARTING OF
BARON BOLLIGREW

ROBERT BOLT

THE THWARTING OF BARON BOLLIGREW

A Play in Two Acts

HEINEMANN
EDUCATIONAL

Heinemann Educational Publishers
Halley Court, Jordan Hill, Oxford OX2 8EJ
a division of Reed Educational & Professional Publishing Ltd
OXFORD   MELBOURNE   AUCKLAND
JOHANNESBURG   BLANTYRE   GABORONE
IBADAN   PORTSMOUTH (NH) USA   CHICAGO

ISBN 0 435 23103 0

*All rights whatsoever in this play are strictly reserved
and on no account should rehearsals commence for a
production unless permission has been obtained*

Professional companies should apply to:
Margaret Ramsay Ltd,
14a Goodwin's Court,
London, W.C.2

Amateur companies should apply to:
Samuel French Limited,
52 Fitzroy Street
London W1P 6JR

Printed in England by Clays Ltd, St Ives plc

FOR JOANNA

SCENERY, PROPS, MUSIC and SOUND

No scenery, just drapes and cyclorama; but there should be good props and costumes. The Church is a model and commences with the 'ruin' which consists of the foundations and the tower, mounted on runners so that it can be dragged about the stage and able to bear the weight of MAGPIE in the nest which tops it. It is completed by four or five smaller segments constructed to fit into place.

MUSIC and SOUND from speakers in the auditorium are openly artificial and exaggerated.

PEOPLE IN THE PLAY

STORYTELLER
Should wear something unique, to set him apart.

DUKE
Elderly, well-fed aristocrat, well meaning and indolent. Wears civilian garb, fairy-tale period.

KNIGHTS
Wear armour, except for JUNIPER, who wears less magnificent civvies than Duke. Surcoats bearing the Royal Strawberry.

SIR OBLONG FITZ OBLONG
Short, plump, pink innocent face topped by tonsure of white hair; pedantic and almost priggy, wears silver armour.

CAPTAIN
Heavy proletarian; rough salt.

JASPER, 15TH BARON BOLLIGREW
Small but burly; red face, black whiskers; choleric and selfish but with the fascination of childish greed. Anachronistically dressed in loud check jacket, bowler hat, breeches, gaiters, carries twelve-bore.

SQUIRE BLACKHEART
Huge and stupid. Wears black armour topped by enormous black plumes.

PEASANTS

Bare-foot, dressed in ragged clothes of sacking.

MEN-AT-ARMS

Conventional Medieval costume, surcoats bearing the golden toad of the Bolligrews.

LORD MAYOR

Timid. Wears slightly less ragged peasant costume, with shoes, and topped by waistcoat and Chain of Office.

MOLOCH

Snappish intellectual. Wears Academic gown.

MAGPIE

Life-like costume of pied feathers. Excitable and amoral.

MAZEPPA

Identical with MAGPIE.

DRAGON

(*Voice only*) Languorous, upper-class, sinister.

CHARACTERS

The Storyteller
The Duke
Sir Digby Vayne-Trumpington
Sir Graceless Strongbody
Sir Percival Smootheley-Smoothe
Sir Oblong Fitz Oblong
Juniper
First Knight
A Captain
Jasper, 15th Baron Bolligrew
Squire Blackheart
First man-at-Arms
Second Man-at-Arms
The Lord Mayor
Obidiah, a Peasant
1st Peasant
2nd Peasant
3rd Peasant
4th Peasant
5th Peasant
Magpie
Secretary
Dr Moloch
Mazeppa
The Dragon
A Corporal
A Cook
A Drummer
A Cymbalist

THE THWARTING OF
BARON BOLLIGREW

ACT ONE

Curtain rises on a stage dark but for a single vertical spot in which stands the STORYTELLER.

STORYTELLER: A long time ago – in the days when dragons were still common – there lived a Duke. And whenever news was brought in of a dragon ravaging some part of the country the Duke sent one of his Knights away in shining armour to deal with it. After a few weeks the Knight would return with the tip of the dragon's tail to prove that he had killed it. Dragon's are excessively vain, and when the tips of their tails are cut off they die, of mulligrubs. The return of the Knights would be announced like this:

Fanfare. Lights up revealing DUKE *and Knights at round table.* Sir Digby Vayne – Trumpington!

Enter TRUMPINGTON.

DUKE: Ah, there you are, Trumpington. Glad to have you back. Got the tip of the dragon's tail?

TRUMPINGTON *places the bright blue tail-tip on table.* DUKE *inspects it.*

Not very big, is it?

TRUMPINGTON: It was not a large dragon, Your Grace, no; but singularly vicious.

IST KNIGHT: They can be tricky, those little blue beggars.

Murmur of agreement.

DUKE: Not complaining, Trumpington. We can't all be St Georges, can we?

While TRUMPINGTON *sits, fanfare.*

STORYTELLER: Sir Graceless Strongbody!

Pause, all looking off expectantly.

DUKE (*indulgently*): Likes to make an entrance, Strongbody . . . (*Pause continuing, less indulgently.*) Call him again.

STORYTELLER: Sir Grace—!

Enter STRONGBODY *dragging huge green tail. Murmur of appreciation and then polite clapping from knights.*

DUKE: I must say, Graceless! I think we'll have this stuffed, gentlemen. How d'you do it?

STRONGBODY (*gruffly*): Oh, usual methods, ye know.

DUKE: Aha – 'Deeds not Words', the old Strongbody motto.
Fanfare.

STORYTELLER: Sir Percival Smoothely-Smoothe!

Enter SMOOTHE.

DUKE: Good show, Smoothe; back on time as usual. Find your dragon?

SMOOTHE *puts down two red tail-tips.*

Good Lord, *two* dragons!

SMOOTHE: No, Your Grace, one dragon with two tails.

DUKE: Well I never saw such a thing in my life. Gave you a bit of trouble I dare say?

SMOOTHE (*sitting*): Not really, Your Grace. It seemed to be confused.

DUKE: Ah, modest, modest. I like that, Smoothe, like it. Well now, who's missing? (*The seat on his left is still vacant.*) Oh, Oblong. Not like him to be late. Well we'll just wait for

Oblong, gentlemen, and then I have a little announcement to make, yes—

Fanfare.

STORYTELLER: Sir Oblong Fitz Oblong!

Enter OBLONG, *sadly.*

DUKE: There you are, Oblong, mission accomplished?

OBLONG: Yes, Your Grace.

DUKE: Got the tail?

OBLONG: Yes, Your Grace.

DUKE (*kindly*): Well perk up, man. Whatever's the matter?

OBLONG (*producing tail*): It was a very small dragon. Your Grace. Small and, er pink. I don't think it can have been fully grown. It meant no harm I'm sure. (*Regards small pink tail on table takes handkerchief from sleeve of armour and blows nose.*)

DUKE: Now Oblong, we all know how you feel about animals, and I'm sure respect you for it. (*Looks round; murmur of confirmation from Knights.*) But – Duty First, eh?

OBLONG (*bracing*): Yes, Your Grace.

DUKE: That's it (*patting* OBLONG'*s shoulder as he sits.*) Never knew an Oblong hold back in the face of duty. (*Briskly.*) Now, Juniper my dear chap, read the next item on the agenda will you?

JUNIPER: Er, Activities for the coming Season, Your Grace.

DUKE: Exactly! (*Rising.*) Gentlemen, a happy announcement: There *are* no activities for the coming season. These (*points to the tails on the table*) were the last dragons in the Dukedom. Thanks to your untiring efforts over the years our peasantry may now reap their harvests – and pay their taxes – without interference. Our towns-folk can make their profits – and pay their taxes – freely. And in short, there isn't a blessed thing for us to do.

KNIGHTS *rise and congratulate one another noisily shaking hands, patting backs, etc. Hubbub dies and all sit.*

OBLONG: How perfectly splendid, Your Grace.

DUKE: Isn't it, isn't it?

OBLONG: Now we can move on somewhere else.

DUKE (*faintly*): . . . Er, 'move on', Oblong?

OBLONG: Yes, Your Grace.

DUKE: Whatever for?

OBLONG (*mildly puzzled*): To succour the poor and needy, Your Grace. Up north, for instance – dragons, barons, goblins. Having a very thin time of it up north, the poor and needy.

DUKE: But my dear fellow – the climate!

OBLONG: Well, south, then, Your Grace.

SMOOTHE (*gently*): May I say something, Your Grace?

DUKE: Smoothe! Yes! please, please.

SMOOTHE: Well gentlemen, we've put this district into some sort of shape – and it's not been easy as you know. It seems to me we've earned a breather.

DUKE: Earned a breather. Well said, Smoothe. Late lie-in in the morning. Bit of jousting in the afternoon perhaps. Substantial supper; jolly good game of musical bumps and off to bed. (*Appealing all round.*) Where's the harm in that?

  Murmur of considered agreement.

I'll put it to the vote. Democratic procedure – Can't say fairer than that, Oblong. All those in favour of the programme just outlined, please say 'Aye'.

ALL BUT OBLONG: Aye!

DUKE: Thank you. All those in favour of moving on to wild, wet, baron and dragon infested areas, please say 'Aye'.

OBLONG: Er, Aye.

DUKE (*cheerfully*): Well there it is, old man. You're outvoted.

OBLONG (*diffident*): Under the terms of our Charter, Your Grace, I *think* a vote on this subject has to be unanimous. Nobody must disagree.

DUKE (*weakly*): That right?

JUNIPER: I'm just looking . . . Yes, here it is, Your Grace, Clause Seven . . . (*Passing Charter to* DUKE.)

DUKE: Well . . . (*Petulant.*) Very ill-judged Clause, I would say. Now what?

JUNIPER: If we can't agree, Your Grace, we must refer the matter to the Royal Court.

STRONGBODY (*gloomily*): And we know what they'll say. . . .

OBLONG: I'm sorry to be the fly in the ointment, gentlemen, but – to succour the poor and needy – dash it all gentlemen, it's our Knightly Vow!

At this, all look uncomfortably at the table. The small pink tail twitches slowly in the silence. All look. OBLONG *distressed.*

Oh dear; Your Grace, would you mind—

DUKE (*testy*): Yes, yes, take it away if it upsets you: take them *all* away.

OBLONG (*muttering embarrassed*): 'Scuse me, gentlemen . . .
I . . . (*going, turns apologetic*) . . . er . . . oh dear. . . .

Exit OBLONG *with tails, watched by all.*

JUNIPER: Well there goes the late lie-in.

STRONGBODY: And the joustin'.

TRUMPINGTON: And the musical bumps.

JUNIPER: And the substantial suppers.

IST KNIGHT (*uneasy*): 'Got a point there, you know, about the Knightly Vow.

DUKE: Yes, yes; capital creature; heart of gold; but . . .

SMOOTHE: But inclined to be dogmatic, Your Grace.

DUKE: Exactly.

SMOOTHE: I think I see a possible solution.

All raise heads, look to SMOOTHE.

Supposing Oblong were to leave us. On a mission. A mission to – say – the Bolligrew Islands.

DUKE: The Bolligrew Islands!

1ST KNIGHT: I say, that's a bit steep.

TRUMPINGTON: D'you think he'd go?

JUNIPER: It's worth trying. Your Grace might have him appointed a Royal Knight Errant.

DUKE: And then when he'd gone we could put the matter to the vote again and – er—?

JUNIPER: And nobody would disagree!

DUKE: Unanimous vote, as required by our Charter!

SMOOTHE: Exactly, Your Grace.

DUKE (*solemnly*): There's no doubt, gentlemen, the Bolligrew Islands *need* a Knight Errant.

JUNIPER: Unquestionably.

DUKE: And Oblong is the obvious choice.

1ST KNIGHT: That's true.

DUKE: I dare say he'll be very happy there.

SMOOTHE *coughs warningly and enter* OBLONG.

Oblong my dear chap, what would you say to the idea of a mission to the Bolligrew Islands?

OBLONG: I should say it was a very *good* idea, Your Grace! When do we start?

DUKE: Well, we were thinking of a – more of a one-man mission, you know.

OBLONG: Oh . . . Me?

DUKE: Yes. Smoothe here suggested you.

OBLONG (*sharply*): Very good of you, Smoothe. I'm not going.

DUKE: 'Not', Oblong?

OBLONG: No! The Bolligrew Islands! That's where Baron Bolligrew lives – the one that pulled down the church!

DUKE (*shocked*): Did he really? I didn't know that.

OBLONG: Well he did. And there's that dragon in the Bolligrew Islands too.

SMOOTHE: A very *poor* specimen, I believe.

OBLONG: It isn't. It's one of those black ones with red eyes.

IST KNIGHT (*uncomfortably*): It's a bit steep, you know.

SMOOTHE: Quite right, quite right. We ought not to persuade Sir Oblong.

OBLONG *making for chair is arrested by*

It is a pity, though. I understand that Baron Bolligrew hunts.

OBLONG (*sharply*): Hunts?

SMOOTHE (*looking up in mock surprise*): Er, hunts, yes.

OBLONG (*suspicious*): What does he hunt?

SMOOTHE: Pretty well anything, they say . . . (*Looking to* DUKE.)

DUKE: Foxes.

SMOOTHE (*nodding*): Foxes, bears . . .

TRUMPINGTON: Deer . . .

JUNIPER: Badgers . . .

OBLONG: Oh the villain!

SMOOTHE (*offhand*): Hares, of course – little, trembling hares . . .

OBLONG: It – really it makes one's blood boil!

SMOOTHE: Your Grace, if Sir Oblong *were* going on this mission I expect His Majesty would make him a Royal Knight Errant, don't you?

DUKE: Couldn't refuse. And then you could wear the purple robe, you know, with the Royal Coat of Arms and so

on. I think Oblong would look well in purple, don't you,
Juniper?

JUNIPER: I've always thought purple would be just the thing.

OBLONG (*taken with it*): Really . . .? I must say . . . Hares and
badgers you say?

SMOOTHE: Oh anything.

OBLONG: The perfect brute! Your Grace, I'll go.

DUKE: Excellent conclusion to a good morning's work,
gentlemen! How about a little refreshment?

STORYTELLER: Lemonade and ice-cream on the South
Terrace!

DUKE: Meeting adjourned!

Exit DUKE *and* KNIGHTS, *rolling round table with them
Lights off but for single spot on* STORYTELLER.

STORYTELLER: So Sir Oblong was appointed a Royal
Knight Errant and at length—

Brown paper parcel thrown on from wings, caught by STORY-
TELLER.

– a parcel from the King's Court arrived at the Duke's
Castle—

Opens it.

– containing Sir Oblong's purple robe.

OBLONG *enters spot, assisted into robe by* STORYTELLER.
Sir Oblong put it on and he found a berth on a ship—

Enter CAPTAIN, *carrying 'mast and sail'.*

– which was making the short but dangerous passage to the
Bolligrew Islands.

CAPTAIN *and* OBLONG *traverse the stage; lightning flash and
thunderclap, in cover of which exit* STORYTELLER. *Lights up.*

OBLONG: These are the Bolligrew Islands are they, Captain?

CAPTAIN: Yus. 'Orrible aren't they? See that ruin up there?

That's the church Baron Bolligrew pulled down some years
back.

OBLONG: He's a difficult man to get on with, I believe.

CAPTAIN: 'Orrible. That's not the worst of it neither.

OBLONG: No?

CAPTAIN: No. See that 'illside; all black and smoky like?

OBLONG: Oh yes.

CAPTAIN: Dragon.

OBLONG: I beg your pardon?

CAPTAIN: Dragon done it. Breathin' fire like. 'Orrible.

OBLONG: Doesn't Baron Bolligrew do anything about it?

CAPTAIN: Not 'im. 'Untin's all 'e cares about. 'Untin' and
grindin' the faces of the poor. Reg'lar terror. You thinkin' of
settlin' 'ere?

OBLONG: Er, well I was, yes ...

CAPTAIN: Wouldn't live 'ere for a million pounds myself.
'Ere we are, 'owever. If you'll just stand on one side, sir.
Ava-a-a-ast! *Bel*-a-a-ay!

    CAPTAIN *pulls cord, sail furls.*

There you are sir, now you can go ashore and—

    Crash of shotgun off.

Look out! 'Ere 'e is.

    Enter BOLLIGREW *carrying shotgun. Walks deliberately to
them. He is accompanied by* BLACKHEART *who moons stolidly
throughout interview, chewing moustache.*

BOLLIGREW: Missed 'im. You Captain Asquith of the ship
Winkle?

CAPTAIN: Yes, me lord.

BOLLIGREW: You brought me new whip?

CAPTAIN: Yes, me lord.

BOLLIGREW: New spurs?

CAPTAIN: Yes, me lord.

BOLLIGREW: New boots?

CAPTAIN: Boots, me lord?

BOLLIGREW: Yes, boots. Me new ridin' boots.

CAPTAIN: They didn't say nothin' about no boots, me lord.

BOLLIGREW: Ho, didn't they?

CAPTAIN: No, me lord.

BOLLIGREW: Well you go back and get 'em.

CAPTAIN (*glancing fearfully back at the 'voyage' just made*): But me lord—

BOLLIGREW: Don't argue with *me*, Asquith. Just turn your ship round and get me boots.

CAPTAIN: Yes, me lord.

    CAPTAIN *hoists sail and exits to more thunder and lightning watched by all.*

BOLLIGREW: Insolent beggar. . . . Who might you be?

OBLONG: Oblong Fitz Oblong.

BOLLIGREW: Gentleman?

OBLONG: Yes?

BOLLIGREW: Me friend, Squire Blackheart.

BLACKHEART: 'D'you do?

OBLONG: How—

BOLLIGREW: Knight Errant, eh?

OBLONG: Yes. (*Modestly.*) A recent appointment.

BOLLIGREW: Knight Errant, Blackheart.

    BLACKHEART *grunts, nods gloomily.*

  D'you hunt?

OBLONG: Well, as a matter of—

BOLLIGREW: I do.

OBLONG: Yes, I hear you're a keen sportsman, Baron.

BOLLIGREW: Keen sportsman. Right. (*Lugging out enormous*

gold watch.) See that? 'Presented to the Master of the
Bolligrew Hounds' – that's me, of course 'as a mark of
admiration and gratitude, by the Chairman of the Hunt
Committee'. Handsome timepiece, eh?

OBLONG: Lovely. Who is the Chairman of the Hunt
Committee?

BOLLIGREW: I am. Solid gold that watch. Had to evict
three or four entire families to pay for it, didn't we
Blackheart?

BLACKHEART: Mm.

BOLLIGREW: Blackheart does all the evictin' work round
here. (*Replacing watch.*) Well. Give you a day tomorrow if
you like.

OBLONG: Baron Bolligrew, I do not hunt!

Short silence.

BOLLIGREW: Doesn't hunt, Blackheart.

BLACKHEART *grunts, nods gloomily.*

(*To* OBLONG.) Afraid of horses, very likely.

OBLONG (*stiffly*): Some of my best friends are horses . . .

BOLLIGREW: Feller's potty, Blackheart.

BLACKHEART: Hey!

BOLLIGREW: What?

BLACKHEART: Magpie.

BOLLIGREW *raises gun. All follow flight of unseen bird above,*
then OBLONG *'accidentally' steps backwards onto* BOLLIGREW'*,*
foot. BOLLIGREW *roars and gun roars.* BOLLIGREW *hopss*
furious, watched apprehensively by OBLONG. BLACKHEART,
oblivious, continues to watch flight of bird, off.

BOLLIGREW (*eyeing* OBLONG *narrowly*): Did you do that on
purpose? He did that on purpose, Blackheart.

BLACKHEART (*lowering his gaze to* BOLLIGREW): What?

BOLLIGREW: He trod on me toe. (*Still eyeing* OBLONG *narrowly.*) Now, look here, Oblong, if you don't 'unt, what've you come for?

OBLONG (*searching armour for paper*): I have my instructions somewhere . . . (*Putting on spectacles.*) . . . It's all pretty run-of-the-mill stuff. (*Clears throat.*) Item: rebuild Bolligrew Island Church. Item: Restore justice to Bolligrew Island Magistrates Court. Item: Suppress Bolligrew Island Dragon.

BOLLIGREW *listens with mounting indignation but now laughs.*

BOLLIGREW: Suppress—? Feller's goin' to suppress the dragon, Blackheart!

BLACKHEART *grins, grin broadens, breaks into guffaws.*

And – and – restore justice to – to the Magistrates Court!

They hold on to one another helpless.

(*To* OBLONG, *wiping his eyes.*) HERE; here – you like to see the Court in session?

OBLONG: At the earliest opportunity, Baron.

BOLLIGREW: Nothing easier.

He takes whistle from pocket and blows. Enter ragged PEASANTRY, also two MEN-AT-ARMS with bench which they put down.

Ready, Blackheart old man?

BLACKHEART: Ready when you are, my dear feller.

They sit.

There you are, Oblong. Court's in session.

OBLONG sits.

BOLLIGREW: What the blazes do you think you're doing?

OBLONG: I am taking my seat on the Bench, Baron.

BOLLIGREW: And who the blazes gave you a seat on the Bench?

OBLONG: My Royal Commission gives me a seat on the Bench, Baron.

BOLLIGREW: Oh. (*Recovering.*) Well, that's all right. We don't mind, do we, Blackheart?

BLACKHEART: Don't we?

BOLLIGREW: No. Loyal subjects of His Majesty, Blackheart and me, Oblong – hope you'll notice that. Right – First Case!

    MEN-AT-ARMS *seize diminutive* PEASANT.

MAN-AT-ARMS: *First* case!

PEASANT (*fearfully*): Here, my lord.

2ND MAN-AT-ARMS: First case present, my lord!

BOLLIGREW: What's the charge?

MAN-AT-ARMS: On the last day of last month, my lord, at about tea-time, prisoner was seen to prevent a horse from eating a double row of runner beans in 'is garden.

BOLLIGREW: Oh. But look here, why *should* he let horses eat his runner beans?

MAN-AT-ARMS: (*slightly shocked*): 'Twas your horse, my lord.

BOLLIGREW: Was it! Guilty!

OBLONG: *Not* guilty!

BOLLIGREW: Squire Blackheart, what do you think?

BLACKHEART: Guilty. Definitely.

BOLLIGREW: That's two to one. Seven days bread and water and – let's see, prisoner aren't you the one with the strawberry bed?

PEASANT: I 'ave got a few strawberry plants, my lord, yes—

BOLLIGREW: Good – and a fine of three baskets of strawberries. You can deliver them to the Castle – back door mind – after you've served your sentence. Next case.

MAN-AT-ARMS: Here, my lord.

BOLLIGREW: You?

MAN-AT-ARMS: Yes, my lord.

BOLLIGREW: But that's one of your men, isn't it Blackheart?

BLACKHEART (*affixing monocle*): It is. It's my Second Hunts-man.

BOLLIGREW: Who's had the blazin' impudence to charge this man?

LORD MAYOR (*timidly determined*): Er, me, my lord.

BOLLIGREW: You Lord Mayor? Well, I can only say that I'm surprised.

LORD MAYOR: My lord, if you feel that my bringing the case is in any way disrespectful, of course—

BOLLIGREW (*holds up a solemn hand*): This is a Court of Law. Case is brought now, Lord Mayor, and must just go forward for an impartial hearing. So let's hear whatever cock-and-bull story you've cooked up.

LORD MAYOR: Well, yesterday morning, my lord, I was in my sweet-shop when I saw this fellow coming along the High Street with a number of dogs.

BLACKHEART: Hounds, Lord Mayor. We call 'em hounds.

LORD MAYOR: Hounds. Thank you. (*Clears throat, continues to* BOLLIGREW.) He came into my shop, took down a jar of best quality humbugs and gave them to these hounds . . .!

BLACKHEART (*brow clearing*): Oh that's all right, Lord Mayor! Wouldn't do 'em any harm. Hounds like humbugs. Often noticed it myself.

LORD MAYOR (*querulous*): Very well, Squire; if you can afford to give your hounds best quality humbugs at four-pence a quarter, very well. But my point is this – do you think your man paid for them? He did not. (*Shrill.*) He never does!

BOLLIGREW (*weakly*): Blackheart, I don't think I can be followin'. Is he suggestin' that your man should *pay* for his humbugs.

BLACKHEART: That your point, Lord Mayor?

LORD MAYOR: It is, Squire, yes.

BLACKHEART: Seems to be a deuced ugly spirit about, old man.

BOLLIGREW: Well I - I'm dumbfounded, Blackheart. I leave it to you.

BLACKHEART: Case dismissed.

BOLLIGREW: Yes? Very well, then. Lord Mayor, I personally take the gravest possible view of this incident. But in the light of my colleague's recommendation to mercy and your hitherto excellent record, I will dismiss you with a caution. Next case!

OBLONG: But this is scandalous!

BOLLIGREW (*nodding, humbly*): You're probably right, Oblong. I tell you frankly, I'm too soft-hearted to be a good Magistrate. (*Jovial.*) Ah - it's you, Bobblenob. Brought me money?

OBIDIAH: No, my lord . . . (*He kneels.*) Mercy . . .

OBLONG: Will somebody please tell me the circumstances of this case?

BOLLIGREW: Ah yes. The circumstances my dear chap are as follows: About ten months ago this man, Obidiah Bobblenob, wilfully and maliciously chucked half a brick through one of my greenhouses—

OBIDIAH: No my lord! Beg pardon my lord, but I didn't, really I didn't!

BOLLIGREW: You see the sort of chap he is, Oblong; thoroughly hardened character; refuses to admit it even now. Without the slightest provocation he pitches a brick through my greenhouse. And what did I do? I fined 'im a pound. One miserable pound. I think you'll agree I was lenient.

OBLONG: How do you make your living, Obidiah?

OBIDIAH: I'm an egg-painter by trade, sir. I sells 'ard-boiled eggs in the market, with designs and funny faces painted on them in different colours.

BOLLIGREW: And a very profitable line it is, as I expect you know!

OBLONG: Then did you pay your fine?

OBIDIAH: No sir, I couldn't!

OBLONG: Why not?

BOLLIGREW: It's a funny thing is that. It seems he had his eggs all ready for market, and the night before some hooligan broke into his cottage and smashed 'em up. That's right, isn't it, Bobblenob?

OBIDIAH (whispers): Yes, my lord.

BOLLIGREW: Mm. So you see, Oblong, when the next Court came round he couldn't pay. However, I wasn't disposed to be hard on him – the Bobblenobs have lived on the estate for generations. Pretty little house Bobblenob lives in . . . got a pond in the garden, hasn't it, Bobblenob?

OBIDIAH: Yes, my lord.

BOLLIGREW: Yes . . . (Briskly.) So all I did was to add another pound to the fine, and leave it at that. (He smiles complacently at OBLONG, as one expecting approval.)

OBLONG: So then he owed you two pounds.

BOLLIGREW (calculating): Er, one and one – two. Yes, exactly two pounds.

OBLONG: And then what?

BOLLIGREW: Well, Oblong, it's an extraordinary thing but the same thing happened again.

OBLONG: So he couldn't pay the fine again.

BOLLIGREW: Exactly—

OBLONG: So you added another pound—

BOLLIGREW: Making three.

OBLONG: And then it happened again.

BOLLIGREW: You're right, my dear chap; it did!

OBLONG: And it's gone on happening ever since.

BOLLIGREW: My dear Oblong, what a brain you must have!

OBLONG: And who is this mysterious 'hooligan' who breaks in and smashes Obidiah's eggs every day before market day, so that he can't pay his fine on Court day?

BOLLIGREW: I've no idea. Have you Bobblenob?

OBIDIAH (*fractional hesitation*): No my Lord.

BOLLIGREW: Well now: It's nine so far so today makes it ten. Nice round number. Ten pounds next Court, Bobblenob. Let's see, there's a market tomorrow morning, isn't there? We'll have a special Court for you that afternoon. And see what you can do at the market, there's a good chap.

OBIDIAH (*whispers*): Yes, my lord.

BOLLIGREW: That's it. I'm relying on you, Bobblenob to save me from a painful duty.

Digs BLACKHEART *in the ribs and laughs.* BLACKHEART *stares at him woodenly.* BOLLIGREW *stops laughing, turns to* OBLONG, *sighs.*

I'm wasted on Black'eart, I really am. Well – Last Case?

MAN-AT-ARMS: *Last* case, my Lord!

BOLLIGREW: Court will rise—!

He and BLACKHEART *rise, then* OBLONG.

And you can all clear off.

Exit hurriedly, all but BLACKHEART, BOLLIGREW *and* OBLONG, MEN-AT-ARMS *taking bench.* BOLLIGREW *takes a cigar from pocket, lights it. Insolently.*

Got the picture?

OBLONG: I have indeed.

BOLLIGREW (*nodding sympathetic*): There's nothing you can do here, Oblong. Go back where you came from, eh?

OBLONG: Baron, Squire – I wish you good-day. (*Going.*)

BOLLIGREW: Oblong!

   OBLONG *turns.* BOLLIGREW *approaches, pointing at him, warningly.*

I've a short way with Knights Errant.

OBLONG: Well, I've a fairly short way with Barons. Good-day.

   Exit OBLONG. BOLLIGREW *looks after him thoughtfully. He turns and looks at* BLACKHEART. BLACKHEART *is mindlessly gazing over audience, sucking one end of his moustache.* BOLLIGREW *approaches him.*

BOLLIGREW: Blackheart. Have a cigar.

BLACKHEART: Mm? Oh, thanks.

BOLLIGREW (*lighting his cigar*): We shall have trouble with that feller, Blackheart.

BLACKHEART: Little fat feller just now?

BOLLIGREW: That's the one. He, er— (*Takes* BLACKHEART *by the elbow; they patrol front stage, smoking cigars.*) He fancies himself as a bit of a fighter for one thing.

BLACKHEART (*interested*): Oh?

BOLLIGREW: Mm. Didn't you notice how he kept lookin' at you?

BLACKHEART: No?

BOLLIGREW: Oh.

BLACKHEART (*anxious*): How was he lookin' at me?

BOLLIGREW: Well you know, like he thought you were a big bag of wind.

BLACKHEART: What?

BOLLIGREW: Mm, you know – like he thought you were a big feller but not much good in a scrap.

BLACKHEART: He didn't!

BOLLIGREW: He did. I wondered how you could put up with it. 'How does Blackheart put up with it,' that's what I kept wonderin'. I mean it's not the thing, is it, for a gentleman to put up with that?

BLACKHEART: I'll flatten 'im! (*Going.*)

BOLLIGREW: Er – Blackheart.

> BLACKHEART *turns.*
>
> BOLLIGREW *beckons him back.*

There *is* a complication.

BLACKHEART: Oh?

BOLLIGREW: Mm. This feller's a Royal Knight Errant ye see. Got the purple mantle.

BLACKHEART: *I'm* not afraid of—

BOLLIGREW: No, no, no – of course you're not. But – we could have trouble from the mainland you see. I mean, we don't want a Royal Commission, do we? I mean, we don't want the Islands *swarming* with Knights Errant, poking their long noses into every blazin' thing, do we?

BLACKHEART (*sobered*): Goo' Lor' no . . . Better leave 'im alone, eh?

BOLLIGREW: Mmm – don't know about that. You *are* a gentleman.

BLACKHEART (*laughing*): Well, I should 'ope so!

BOLLIGREW: Yes. Well then, you're entitled to satisfaction. But, just make sure you do it in the proper form.

BLACKHEART: Right. (*Glances off, uneasy; draws close to* BOLLIGREW.) What *is* the proper form?

BOLLIGREW: Oh. Well. First, you must throw down the gauntlet.

BLACKHEART (*gazing at it*): Me gauntlet.

BOLLIGREW: That's it. Chuck it down. That's a challenge. Then if he picks it up—

BLACKHEART: Yes?

BOLLIGREW: You can clobber him.

BLACKHEART: Right.

BOLLIGREW: If he *don't* pick it up—

BLACKHEART: Yes?

BOLLIGREW: Then insult him. And if he *still* won't fight—

BLACKHEART: Yes?

BOLLIGREW: Then you can't touch him.

BLACKHEART: Well what's the good of that?

BOLLIGREW: Ah. You see, old man, you must do it in front of witnesses. This fellar, ye see, has set himself up as the Champion of the poor and needy. And if 'e won't fight after *that*—

BLACKHEART: Yes?

BOLLIGREW: Well then, his sweaty friends will see what sort of Champion they've got! Won't they?

BLACKHEART (*grunts*): Yes, but look 'ere, where's me satisfaction?

BOLLIGREW: That, Blackheart, would satisfy any gentleman that ever breathed.

BLACKHEART: Oh. Right. Let's have it again. That's gauntlet, insult, sweaty...?

BOLLIGREW (*looks at him dubiously*): Tell you what. Come up to the castle and I'll jot it down for you.

BLACKHEART: Oh. Right.

As they are going, enter STORYTELLER, *struggling with Church ruins.*

BOLLIGREW: Evening.

STORYTELLER: Good evening, Baron.

BOLLIGREW: What you got there then?

STORYTELLER: The ruins of Bolligrew Church, Baron. We shall need them for the next scene.

BOLLIGREW: Church ruins, Blackheart. Thought they looked familiar.

STORYTELLER (*pausing, breathless*): I wonder if the Squire would—?

BLACKHEART: My good man, I'm not a bally labourer.

BOLLIGREW: Quite right. You got any heavin' and liftin' to do, find a bally peasant!

Exit BLACKHEART *and* BOLLIGREW. STORYTELLER *calls off.*

STORYTELLER: Sir Oblong!

Enter OBLONG.

STORYTELLER: I wonder if you'd—

OBLONG: Of course.

They lug the ruins into place.

Church ruins, eh?

STORYTELLER: Yes, we need them for the next scene.

OBLONG: Mm, pretty. Must have been a pretty little place – I shall enjoy the first part of my mission. (*Anxious.*) However, I shall need assistance . . .

STORYTELLER: The poor and needy?

OBLONG: Excellent.

STORYTELLER *addresses audience.*

STORYTELLER: The poor and needy of the Island, when they heard that he had come to be their champion, flocked in upon the gallant Knight from every side!

Enter PEASANTS, LORD MAYOR. OBLONG *addresses them.*

OBLONG: Poor and needy, Lord Mayor. I have been sent here by the Duke to help you. Will you help me?

Dubious agreement from PEASANTS.

PEASANTS: Don't see why not—
   Give it a go—
   'pends what kind of 'elp 'e wants.

OBLONG: In the first place I want information. Tell me something about Squire Blackheart. (*He notes down their replies.*)

1ST PEASANT: 'E's a 'ard case is the Squire, sir.

2ND PEASANT: You know that black armour of his, sir?

OBLONG: Yes?

2ND PEASANT: Never takes it off, sir.

3RD PEASANT: 'E sleeps in it.

OBLONG (*noting it all down nodding gravely*): One of those, is he?... Now what about the Dragon?

On the word 'Dragon' PEASANTS *scatter. Stop. Return.*

1ST PEASANT: 'Ere. Don't you go near Dragon, now.

2ND PEASANT: Gobble you up like a raspberry, 'e will.

3RD PEASANT: Baron 'isself is afeared of Dragon.

OBLONG: My understanding was that the Baron has some sort of arrangement with the Dragon.

4TH PEASANT: So 'e 'as, sir. Baron 'as this side of the Island for grindin' the faces of the poor, and Dragon 'as that side of the Island for ravagin'. That's the agreement. But I reckon the Baron be afeared of 'e all the same . . .

OBLONG: Matters here are worse than I had realized. (*Flips shut his notebook.*) Now my first task is to rebuild this church. May I count on your assistance?

1ST PEASANT: Baron isn't goin' to like that, sir.

2ND PEASANT: 'E doan' 'old wi' churches, sir.

3RD PEASANT: I mean, 'e pulled it down; stands to reason 'e doan' want it buildin' up again.

OBLONG: If we are to consult the likes and dislikes of the Baron at every turn, we shall accomplish very little. (*Awkward silence.*) Remember – you will be under the protection of the Duke!

5TH PEASANT: Meanin' no disrespect sir, but Duke's a long way away. We ain't never seen Duke in the Islands, sir.

OBLONG: That is a just observation . . . (*He considers, mounts ruin, addresses them, Crispin's Day fashion.*) There was a time when the peasants of this island were a byword for their fearlessness and sturdy independence! In time of Peace they followed the plough with straight backs and heads high!

PEASANTS *unconsciously straighten backs.*

In time of War—

PEASANTS *unconsciously fall into martial postures.*

– they pressed as though by instinct even to the thickest of the fray, hard after the great banner of the Bolligrew the Golden Toad, and were a terror to the very cream of foreign chivalry!

PEASANTS (*carried away*): Hurrah!

OBLONG: These were your fathers! Are you their sons?

PEASANTS: Yes!

OBLONG: Then do we build the church?

PEASANTS: We do!

OBLONG: Then (*pointing dramatically*) building materials!

PEASANTS: Building materials! (PEASANTS *rush off stage enthusiastically*.)

LORD MAYOR: A wonderful gift for words you have.

OBLONG: Oh it's all part of our training you know. Where do *you* stand in this business?

LORD MAYOR: You understand, Sir Oblong, I'm, er delicately situated.

OBLONG: I do see that.

LORD MAYOR: If there's anything I can do in proper form ...

OBLONG: I understand.

LORD MAYOR: But I can hardly take part in, well, a popular uprising.

OBLONG: You're delicately situated.

LORD MAYOR: Thank you. Er (*he edges closer to* OBLONG) – between ourselves, you've put your finger on the nub of the matter with this fellow Blackheart. Between ourselves (*glancing about*) – not really out of the top drawer.

OBLONG: No?

LORD MAYOR: No. For all his moustaches. His father (*glances around again*) his father was an under footman in the late Lord Bolligrew's time.

OBLONG: Really?

LORD MAYOR: I remember him. I went to school with Squire Blackheart so-called. An inveterate bully, Sir Oblong, and backward in his lessons, very backward ... (*He breaks off as noise of* PEASANTS *approaches. They enter bearing sections of church: one with wheelbarrow, one with stepladder*.)

1ST PEASANT (*breathless*): There you are, sir!

2ND PEASANT: Building materials!

OBLONG: Splendid! (*Inspects contents of wheelbarrow*.) Mortar and trowel. Splendid, splendid. (*Takes handles of barrow*.)

Now then. For your manhood and your ancient liberties. Forward!

He steps out rhetorically with barrow, followed by PEASANTS, *but stops, instantly as: enter* BLACKHEART. *Enter separately,* STORYTELLER, *who watches soberly.*

Good evening, Squire.

BLACKHEART: Tchah!

He advances deliberately, PEASANTS *shrinking back, and hurls down his gauntlet.*

OBLONG: You've dropped your glove.

BLACKHEART: I've thrown down me gauntlet. Any gentleman'd know that.

OBLONG: You want me to fight a duel with you, Squire?

BLACKHEART: Right.

OBLONG: Well, I'm not going to.

BLACKHEART: Then – (*an effort of memory*) – I'm goin' to insult you!

OBLONG: Well please be quick; I have a lot to do and the light's going.

BLACKHEART (*studies a grubby scrap of paper*): Oblong, you're a – a, mm . . . (*He has difficulty in reading.*)

OBLONG *peers at the paper.*

OBLONG: Varlet.

BLACKHEART: Right! A varlet! And a, mm . . .

OBLONG: Knave.

BLACKHEART: That's it! Knave and varlet! You – you're not a gentleman! Thought of that meself.

OBLONG: The subject seems to obsess you, Squire.

BLACKHEART (*amazed*): Well, if you won't fight *now*—

OBLONG: No.

BLACKHEART (*nonplussed, consults paper, brow clears*): Well then, your sweaty friends can see what kind of Champion they've *got*! (*To* 5TH PEASANT.) You.

5TH PEASANT (*approaching, humbly*): Yes, Squire?

BLACKHEART: Pick up me glove.

5TH PEASANT: Yes, Squire. (*Does so.*)

　　Behind OBLONG, PEASANTS *lay down sections of church.*

BLACKHEART (*going, to* OBLONG): And a very good evening to *you*, Fatty!

　　Exit BLACKHEART.

OBLONG (*watching him off*): What a deplorable exhibition! Well now— (*Turns to find* PEASANTS *going.*) What's the matter? Stop!

　　Exit PEASANTS, 5TH PEASANT *passing.*

　　My good friend—

5TH PEASANT: Sorry, sir. But if you'm afeared to tackle Squire, we'm afeared to 'elp you. And that's the top and bottom of it, sir.

　　Exit 5TH PEASANT.

OBLONG (*to* LORD MAYOR): I'm not afraid of the Squire!

LORD MAYOR: No. No. Of course not.

OBLONG: But duelling is utterly against my principles.

LORD MAYOR: I agree with you, Sir Oblong, I agree with you. (*But he is backing towards the Exit.*)

OBLONG: Well, the two of us must just do what we can, eh? (*Attempts to lift large segment of church.*) Would you—?

LORD MAYOR: The fact is, sir, I ought to be getting back to the shop. I'm sorry, Sir Oblong, really I am . . .

　　Exit LORD MAYOR.

OBLONG: Dash it! (*Defiantly.*) Yes – I am not often intemperate in my language but *dash* it! . . . What shall I do now?

STORYTELLER: I'm afraid I can't tell you.

OBLONG: But you're the Storyteller aren't you?

STORYTELLER: I am the Storyteller, yes.

OBLONG: Well what happens next in the story?

STORYTELLER: What happens next, Sir Oblong, is that you are left on your own.

Exit STORYTELLER.

OBLONG: Well that's very inconvenient—!

Appeals to audience.

What shall I do . . .? Perhaps I ought to have fought that fellow Blackheart after all? What do you think?

Continues ad lib till audience response strong.

Might do him good to learn a lesson, eh? In my younger days I was national Broadsword Champion you know, and – and Area Champion three years running!

Growing excited.

After all, he challenged me, didn't he? Perhaps I ought to find the fellow now? Do a little challenging myself? Ha! (*Draws sword.*) Have at thee for a foul caitiff! Take that – and that – anthatanthatanthat!

When response maximum, pulls himself up.

No. No. (*Sheathes sword.*) Certainly not. I have been sent here to set a good example. You ought to be ashamed of yourselves. Duelling, is *wrong* . . . I must manage somehow by myself. (*Attempts to lift segment of church.*) No . . . Now let's see . . . No . . . You know at this point in the story I do think they might send *somebody* to help me.

Enter unseen by him MAGPIE.

However . . . Keep trying . . . No.

VOICE FROM AUDIENCE: Behind you!

OBLONG: What? Try a smaller piece? Right. Now, then . . .

No . . . I really don't see how I'm going to manage, you know . . . How about this bit . . .?

And so on, till audience response strong. Then turns, sees MAGPIE.

OBLONG: Oh. Good evening.

MAGPIE: You talk.

OBLONG: Certainly.

MAGPIE: Most human beings only twitter.

OBLONG: Most human beings would say that most birds only twitter.

MAGPIE: Eh?

OBLONG: Mm. As a matter of fact, all human beings talk, among themselves.

MAGPIE: Don't believe it.

OBLONG: Well that's rather narrow-minded of you. It takes all sorts to make a world you know.

MAGPIE: My name's Mike Magpie. Your name's Oblong. You saved my life this morning.

OBLONG: Oh, was that you?

MAGPIE: Ark.

OBLONG: He might have missed you know.

MAGPIE: Not 'im. You saved my life an' you can count on me.

OBLONG: For what?

MAGPIE: Anything! I'm a pretty smart character.

OBLONG: Are you now?

MAGPIE: Oh yes. Brilliant bird – always have been.

OBLONG: Well the immediate task is to rebuild this church.

MAGPIE: Oh . . . Like, lugging stones about?

OBLONG: Yes?

MAGPIE: Like – work?

OBLONG: Yes, Michael work.

MAGPIE: Well look 'ere, Obby, work's not in my line. **Any-thin' in the thieving line** now, or the telling lies line, or the leading up the garden path line—

OBLONG: Did you say 'thieving'?

MAGPIE: Yes. You know – pinching things.

OBLONG (*quietly*): What things?

MAGPIE: Shiny things. They're in my nest. 'D'you like to see?

OBLONG (*mounting ladder*): Yes Michael, I should.

MAGPIE: Hey! You're not going to take my shiny things, are you?

OBLONG: Yours, Michael? (*Peering into nest.*) Mm. I am on the whole relieved. Silver paper, bits of glass – but here is a silver tie-pin with a fox head on it which appears to be of some value.

MAGPIE: That's all right; that's Bolligrew's!

OBLONG (*descending*): It makes not an atom of difference whose it is. Stealing is *wrong*.

MAGPIE: It's no good talking to me about right and wrong, Obby. It's not in my nature.

OBLONG: I know it's difficult for Magpies, Michael, but I want you to try. Imagine the impression it would make in the Islands if it were thought that I associated with a bird – I am sorry to say this – a bird of loose principles.

MAGPIE: Awk.

OBLONG: No more stealing then.

MAGPIE: Aw—

Noise off.

Awk! A person!

OBLONG: Hide.

MAGPIE *climbs to nest.* OBLONG *peers off, hand on sword. A light approaches.*

Who's that?

Enter OBIDIAH.

OBIDIAH: It's me, sir. Bobblenob the egg painter.

OBLONG: Ah, Obidiah. My poor friend, I'm sorry I wasn't able to help you in Court this morning.

OBIDIAH: You did your best sir, and I thanks you for it. That's what I come to say, sir.

OBLONG: There's no chance of your having the ten pounds by next Court Day, I suppose?

OBIDIAH: How can a poor man like me come by ten pounds, sir?

OBLONG: If I had any money myself I'd give it to you, Obidiah, willingly. But I haven't. We're not allowed to, you know.

OBIDIAH: I know that, sir. I've sometimes thought if Knights Errant were provided with proper funds, sir, they might make more of an impression, sir.

OBLONG: It's not for us to question the regulation, Obidiah.

OBIDIAH: No sir.

OBLONG: Can't you possibly make some eggs to sell at tomorrow's market?

OBIDIAH: I'd need a power of eggs to make ten pounds. And then again it's fiddlin' work, sir, is egg painting, and I couldn't get 'em finished by tomorrow, sir, if I 'ad 'em.

OBLONG: No, I suppose not.

OBIDIAH: And what if I did, sir, they'd only be smashed up again like the others.

OBLONG: Have you no idea who it is that breaks into your cottage and smashes up your eggs?

OBIDIAH: I *know* who it is, sir. It's Squire Blackheart.

OBLONG: Squire Blackheart! Obidiah, do you know what you are saying?

OBIDIAH: I seen 'im at it, sir, plain as I see you. But what can I do with a great strong gentleman like that? Well, sir, you yourself... I mean, you 'esitate don't you?

OBLONG: I hesitate no longer, Obidiah. (*He paces about restlessly.*) I find myself agitated. (*He stops.*) It's Baron Bolligrew who sends him, of course?

OBIDIAH: That's right, sir. 'Tisn't the money he wants, sir. 'Tis my cottage he's after. When he's raised the fine to fifteen pounds or thereabouts 'e'll take the cottage instead.

OBLONG: I see. Or rather, no I don't see. What on earth does Baron Bolligrew want with a cottage?

OBIDIAH: Well, sir; this pond goes with the cottage – and there's trout in this pond, sir.

OBLONG: Aha!

OBIDIAH: Yes, sir. Baron an' Squire been keen fishermen many a year now. Mine be last trout in the Islands near enough. And finer, happier fish you never did see. I feeds 'em night and morning, sir, same as my father did before me. Friends of the family, they are, in a manner of speakin', sir.

OBLONG (*looking at him sharply*): You converse with them, Obidiah?

OBIDIAH: Nothing I likes better of an evening, sir, than a quiet chat with they trout.

OBLONG: Then, Obidiah, I wish you to meet a friend of mine. (*Calls.*) Michael! Will you come here, please? A shrewd bird Bobblenob and knows the Island. Michael Magpie; Obidiah Bobblenob.

MAGPIE: Awk.

OBLONG: Michael, you have heard Obidiah's predicament?

MAGPIE: Awk.

OBLONG: What do you make of it?

MAGPIE: Tricky. How many eggs to make ten quid?

OBIDIAH: Two hundred, seventy-seven.

OBLONG: And then we should have to paint designs on them you see, before tomorrow morning's market.

MAGPIE: Oh *that's* all right – I'm a dab hand with a paint brush.

OBLONG: Really? Mm – it is sad how often talent and deliquency go hand in hand.

MAGPIE: No, the real snag's getting the eggs in the first place . . .

OBLONG: It is indeed . . .

MAGPIE (*suddenly to* OBIDIAH): Hen's eggs?

OBIDIAH: Well, how—?

MAGPIE: Not heron's eggs? Seagull's? Pheasant's? Peewit's?

OBIDIAH: Very tasty, when you can get 'em.

MAGPIE: I can get 'em.

OBIDIAH: Can you?

MAGPIE: Course I can.

OBIDIAH: Two hundred 'seventy seven?

MAGPIE: Easy. Couple each. Can't count, most of 'em.

OBLONG: Michael. There can be no question of *stealing* these eggs from your friends. No, Obidiah, not even for this.

MAGPIE: For this they'll give 'em, Obby.

OBLONG: Will they really?

MAGPIE: If I ask them.

OBLONG: Well there we are then! Hope, Obidiah! Do you begin to hope?

OBIDIAH: I do sir!

OBLONG: You fetch your materials; we will collect the eggs. (*To* MAGPIE.) When can we begin?

MAGPIE: As soon as the moon comes up.

OBLONG: Oh.

Enter STORYTELLER.

Ah. Would you bring the moon up?

White moon ascends; bright moonlight.

Thank you. Now my friends, to work!

Exit OBIDIAH, *left.* OBLONG *and* MAGPIE *right.*

STORYTELLER: For half that night they walked the island from one nest to another, and everywhere they met with success. Some birds gave their eggs because they knew Mike Magpie, many because they took a fancy to Sir Oblong, most because they detested Baron Bolligrew and wished to see him foiled. Some gave one, some gave two, some as many as half a dozen, and by one o'clock in the morning the collection totalled—

Enter OBIDIAH *with implements,* OBLONG *and* MAGPIE *with basket of eggs.*

OBLONG: Two hundred and seventy-seven! Michael my dear Magpie, I have no words to express my admiration for your resourcefulness and the high esteem in which you are evidently held by these excellent birds.

MAGPIE: Awk!

OBLONG: Now, Obidiah we are in your hands. First I suppose we must boil them?

OBIDIAH: It's plain to see you don't know much about egg paintin' sir. First we paints 'em, then we boils 'em; thus preparing the egg itself for consumption and fixin' the colours used in the design. We don't speak of boilin' an egg in the trade, we speaks of fixin' an egg.

OBLONG: How interesting.

OBIDIAH: Yes. I have brought along one of my old books of sample designs.

OBLONG: Very sensible.

> OBLONG *and* MAGPIE *look at book.*

Mm. These look rather ambitious, Obidiah.

OBIDIAH: These (*another book*) are simpler designs for the use of apprentices.

OBLONG: Ah. Ah, that's more like it.

MAGPIE: Pooh. (*Takes other book.*)

OBLONG: Well then, let's commence.

> *All in unison sit, take one egg, dip brush, work.*

STORYTELLER: And so they commenced, each giving of his best according to his own ability. Obidiah Bobblenob produced his usual quota of highly professional eggs, Mike Magpie produced a small number of very ingenious eggs and Sir Oblong a large number of rather elementary eggs, some of which he painted bright blue all over. But when the moon went down and dawn came up, they had done.

> *Moon goes down; light changes, during which* SIR OBLONG *turns basket about, presenting painted side of eggs to audience.*

OBLONG: Done!

OBIDIAH: And I thanks you all from the bottom of my heart.

MAGPIE: I'm tired.

BADGER: Me too.

OBLONG: I'm a bit fatigued myself. However. Now we must boil – er fix – them, I suppose?

OBIDIAH (*settling himself comfortably*): One thing we never does in the trade, sir, is pass straight from the paintin' to the fixin'. The hand is unsteady and the brain excited. Many a

panful of eggs I've seen split from top to bottom by some
unchancy journeyman for lack of forty winks.

OBLONG (*attracted*): Forty winks? Have we time?

MAGPIE *already asleep.*

OBIDIAH: Ample time, sir. Market don't open till ten o'clock.
If we takes 'em down to my cottage at nine o'clock say, we
take 'em straight from the fixin' to the market and – less
chance of runnin' into Squire Blackheart, sir.

OBLONG: That's well thought of. (*Lying down.*) Though I'm
bound to admit I shouldn't mind crossing swords with the
fellow . . . Upon a legitimate occasion . . . Do you know
his father was an under footman?

But OBIDIAH *too, has fallen asleep.* OBLONG *sleeps, hands
clasped on tummy.*

STORYTELLER: Now Squire Blackheart, owing to his habit of
sleeping in his armour, slept little and rose early. On this
particular morning, disturbed by a loose rivet, he rose
particularly early and went for an early morning walk – with
his favourite hound.

Enter BLACKHEART, *front stage, preceded by cut-out hound
on wheels. Walk almost off, double-takes sharply, letting go of
hound which runs off into wings opposite.* BLACKHEART *tiptoes
to the sleepers, inspects them. Sees eggs. Reacts. Looks furtively
off, left and right, draws sword, raises it high in the air, flat side
down, and is about to smash the eggs.*

OBLONG (*still recumbent, opening eye*): Good morning, Squire.

BLACKHEART *checks.* OBLONG *rises.*

What are you doing?

BLACKHEART: What d'you think I'm doin'?

OBLONG: I think you are about to destroy Obidiah's eggs.

BLACKHEART: Right.

OBLONG: Not, I think, for the first time.

BLACKHEART: Right. Out of me way, fatty— (*Pushing* OBLONG.)

OBLONG (*resisting*): One moment. (*Clasps hand behind back.*) Yesterday, Squire, you permitted yourself to insult me. 'Varlet and Knave' I think it was.

BLACKHEART: That's it; varlet and knave. I remember.

OBLONG: Blackheart, it is my considered opinion that you are a commonplace rogue and a disgrace to your profession.

BLACKHEART: *Eh?*

OBLONG: One moment.

Puts his hand under BLACKHEART's *nose, snaps finger and thumb.*

BLACKHEART: A-aaah!

Takes a terrific swipe, which OBLONG *nimbly jumps over.*

OBLONG: Not a bad stroke, Squire. Now—!

OBLONG *draws sword. They fight.* BLACKHEART's *strokes are lethal but ponderous;* OBLONG *fights light-weight style, great dexterity but no knock-out punch.* STORYTELLER *enters and watches calmly. The whistle of* BLACKHEART's *blade and the merry clatter of* OBLONG's *short sword, their gasping breath, are taken up and exaggerated by Speaker.* OBLONG *is borne backwards off stage, followed by* OBIDIAH. MAGPIE *hides behind church with basket as* BLACKHEART *enters.*

BLACKHEART: The eggs! Where are the blazin' eggs?

Enter OBLONG, *limping but determined.*

OBLONG: Come along Squire, we haven't finished.

BLACKHEART *rushes at him. Enter* OBIDIAH *and* MAGPIE *emerges. Avoiding combatants they collide and* MAGPIE *falls.* BLACKHEART *kicks him.* MAGPIE *seizes* BLACKHEART's *leg and nips ankle with beak.*

Michael, let go! One on to one! That's the rule! Let go immediately!

OBLONG *borne off again.* MAGPIE *and* OBIDIAH *exit, swiftly, tiptoes with basket. Noise of battle ceases on cry from* BLACKHEART. *Enter* OBLONG, *breathless.*

I'm getting, getting past it . . . One does not realize.

STORYTELLER: Would perhaps (*nodding discreetly to exit opposite*) discretion be the better part of valour?

OBLONG: Run away? (*He seems tempted for a moment.*) No. There's life, life in the old dog yet.

Enter BLACKHEART, *also limping.*

BLACKHEART: Had enough, have you?

OBLONG: Certainly not. Lay on, and may the best man win!

They fight again. Despite their differing styles, they are well matched but it is OBLONG *who is once again borne off, watched by* STORYTELLER. *Din of battle recedes.* STORYTELLER *walks slowly forward. The noise is now dwindling, goon-fashion, to infinity.*

STORYTELLER: It is sad but true that when men fight, the fight goes not to the best man but to the best fighter.

Lights high.

Enter BOLLIGREW, *in tearing high spirits. Blows whistle.*

BOLLIGREW: Court! Court's in session! Draw near!

Enter MEN-AT-ARMS, PEASANTS, LORD MAYOR, *as before.*

That's the spirit! Ah, there you are Bobblenob! Good market this mornin'? Trade brisk?

OBIDIAH *smiles sadly.*

Ha ha! Just my little joke, you know. (*Sits.*) Well now. (*Surprised.*) Where's me colleague?

MAN-AT-ARMS (*looking off*): Coming now, my lord.

BOLLIGREW (*calls, cheerfully*): Come on, Blackheart, I'm waitin'!

    Enter OBLONG, *limping on stick adhesive plaster on fore-head.*

BOLLIGREW: Oh, it's you. (*Grins.*) Been in an accident, old man?

OBLONG: You might call it that. (*Sitting.*)

BOLLIGREW (*sotto*): Challenged you, did he?

OBLONG (*sotto*): He did challenge me, yes.

BOLLIGREW: Mm. Well, you may think you've had a hiding, but he's let you off pretty lightly – compared to some of the thumpings I've seen him hand out, eh, Corporal?

MAN-AT-ARMS: Yes, my lord; that gentleman 'e 'ad words with at the point-to-point.

BOLLIGREW: Blood all over the paddock.

    BOLLIGREW *and* MEN-AT-ARMS *laugh reminiscently.*

    (*Irritable.*) Wonder where he is?

MAN-AT-ARMS: 'Spect 'e's 'avin' forty winks, sir.

2ND MAN-AT-ARMS: Always likes forty winks after a scrimmage, does the Squire, sir. Makes him sleepy.

BOLLIGREW: Well I'm not waitin'. Bobblenob, stand forward. Oh, it occurs to me, Oblong, that you and I might disagree on the verdict.

OBLONG: Quite likely.

BOLLIGREW: Well, we don't want poor old Bobblenob held up by the delays of Court, do we?

OBLONG: No.

BOLLIGREW: No. So I'll appoint another Magistrate. Corporal, you're a Magistrate. Siddown. I've been thinkin' about this case, Corporal, and I'm afraid I can't let it go on any longer. What do you think?

MAN-AT-ARMS: If 'e don't pay up today, my lord, I should put 'im inside.

BOLLIGREW: That would be *too* severe. But I'm afraid I shall have to take his cottage, you know.

MAN-AT-ARMS: If 'e don't pay up today, my lord, I should take 'is cottage.

BOLLIGREW: That's settled then. Cheer up, Oblong. Bobble-nob's probably *got* the money today! Got the money Bobblenob?

OBIDIAH: Yes, my lord.

BOLLIGREW: Well now, look here, this can't go . . . *Eh?* You have?

OBIDIAH: Yes, my lord. Ten pounds; the proceeds of my painted egg stall this morning.

OBLONG: You seem surprised, Baron?

BOLLIGREW: Surprised? Well I – well – I – we – er—

OBLONG: We did have a little trouble getting the eggs.

BOLLIGREW (*staring at him, hypnotized*): The eggs. Yes, you would.

OBLONG: And then of course the mysterious hooligan turned up.

BOLLIGREW: Oh. The 'ooligan . . .

OBLONG: Yes.

BOLLIGREW: You *beat* him?

OBLONG: With some difficulty, but yes, I think I may say I beat him.

BOLLIGREW (*tears his eyes away from* OBLONG): Well, that's very satisfactory! Congratulations, Bobblenob. Glad your troubles are over. (*Taking the money.*) Court will rise—

BOLLIGREW *and* MAN-AT-ARMS *rise.*

OBLONG: One moment, Baron!

BOLLIGREW (*reluctantly*): Court sit.

  BOLLIGREW *and* MAN-AT-ARMS *sit.*

OBLONG: Baron, I think we can at last establish the identity of this hooligan.

BOLLIGREW (*mopping forehead with handkerchief*): You do?

OBLONG: Yes. He left behind him a piece of tangible evidence.

  He produces the enormous black plume from BLACKHEART's *helmet.*

  Do you know who's it is?

BOLLIGREW (*shaking head vigorously*): Never seen it before.

MAN-AT-ARMS: That's Squire Black'eart's, my lord.

BOLLIGREW: Idiot!

OBLONG: Well I knew it was, of course, but I'm glad to have that confirmed by our colleague on the Bench here. People's exhibit One.

BOLLIGREW: Look here, Obby old man, what exactly are you goin' to do with that?

OBLONG: I thought of sending it to the Duke's High Court on the mainland.

BOLLIGREW: High Court, eh?

OBLONG: Yes. No doubt the Squire will explain to them *why* a gentleman in his position should persecute a humble egg painter. (*As one struck.*) Unless, of course . . .

BOLLIGREW: Yes?

OBLONG: Unless we were to deal with the case in our own little Court here.

BOLLIGREW: I knew you were the right sort, Obby! Just – just give me that thing and – you can rebuild the church!

OBLONG: I shall do that in any case. I was thinking now of the second part of my mission: the restoration of justice here.

BOLLIGREW: Anythin' you say old man.

OBLONG: Well, in the first place, I think Blackheart himself should resign from the Bench.

BOLLIGREW: He's resigned.

OBLONG: And then – (*confidential*) – is the Corporal really suitable? I mean, has he really the legal brain?

BOLLIGREW: Complete fool. He's resigned, too. You've resigned, you numbskull. Get off the Bench!

MAN-AT-ARMS *does so.*

OBLONG: And now, you see, there are just the two of us again.

BOLLIGREW: And very nice too, Obby. Couldn't be happier. Now let's have that, there's a good chap.

OBLONG: You see, there ought to be a third Magistrate in case, as you very shrewdly pointed out, you and I should disagree.

BOLLIGREW (*licking his lips*): A third Magistrate?

OBLONG: What about the Lord Mayor? (*He offers the plume, but* BOLLIGREW'*s hand checks.*)

BOLLIGREW: The—?

OBLONG: Lord Mayor. (*Withdrawing plume.*) Otherside, you see, I don't think we shall be competent to judge this case.

BOLLIGREW (*sinister*): Lord Mayor . . . do you *want* to be a Magistrate?

LORD MAYOR (*nervous giggle*): You see, Sir Oblong, I'm delicately situated.

OBLONG: Baron, persuade him.

BOLLIGREW (*between his teeth*): Lord Mayor, I would take it as a personal favour if you would accept a seat on the Bench!

LORD MAYOR (*another giggle*): Sir Oblong, may we take it that this morning you met Squire Blackheart in personal combat, and, er, defeated him?

OBLONG: Soundly, Lord Mayor.

LORD MAYOR: Then, Baron, I am happy to accept your invitation.

He sits nervously at far end of Bench from BOLLIGREW. OBLONG *offers plume,* BOLLIGREW *snatches it. Glowers.*

BOLLIGREW: Court rise!

He leaps to his feet; LORD MAYOR *half rises.*

OBLONG: The case, Baron.

BOLLIGREW: Eh?

OBLONG (*indicating plume in* BOLLIGREW'*s hands*): The case.

BOLLIGREW: Court sit.

BOLLIGREW *sits, heavily.*

OBLONG: to my mind, gentlemen, those ten pounds belong to Obidiah Bobblenob.

BOLLIGREW (*stares incredulously, then*): No!

OBLONG: Lord Mayor, what do you think?

BOLLIGREW (*grimly*): Yes, Lord Mayor, what *do* you think?

All heads turn to LORD MAYOR; PEASANTS *shuffle forward a step suspense.* LORD MAYOR *licks his lips, grips his knees, avoids* BOLLIGREW'*s glaring eye.*

LORD MAYOR: . . . I agree with Sir Oblong!

OBLONG (*beaming at him*): Well done, Lord Mayor! Very well done indeed! (*Takes money from* BOLLIGREW'*s nerveless hand, gives it to* OBIDIAH.) Case dismissed?

LORD MAYOR (*delighted with himself*): Case dismissed!

OBLONG: That's two to one, Baron.

BOLLIGREW (*snarls*): Case dismissed!

Triumphal march music and cheering pours from speaker; OBLONG *and* LORD MAYOR *rise, cheering* PEASANTS *crowd round.*

OBLONG: To the Church!

He leads the way, circuitously round the stage; PEASANTS

fall in step behind him. In time to the march, the segments of Church are fitted into place. A bell is placed in tower, at which the cheerful pandemonium on Speaker is augmented by Church bells. OBLONG *is carried shoulder high and all exit.* OBLONG *bowing and waving graciously to left and right.* BOLLIGREW *is left slumped sullen and motionless on Bench. Off stage celebration dwindles to silence on Speaker.*

Enter BLACKHEART, *cautiously; he looks nervously to left and right.* BOLLIGREW *turns head and watches him sourly. His plume is missing, bits of his armour have come loose and flap from him, his sword is broken short and sharply bent.*

BLACKHEART: Has he gone?

BOLLIGREW: Ha! Me invincible Champion, battling Black-'eart!

BLACKHEART: Now don't take that tone, Bolligrew! (*Limps to Bench and sits with a clatter. Aggrieved.*) Feller's a professional. Don't fight like a gentleman. Jumps about like a bally grass'opper! Can't get a decent swipe at 'im. Look at me armour – me best suit!

BOLLIGREW (*roars*): And 'oo paid for it, might I ask? 'Oo signed the whackin' great cheque for it?

He rises and soliloquizes, trembling with self-pity.

Here am I, doing no harm to anybody . . . ! Followin' the innocent pursuits of a retired country gentleman . . . ! Along comes this interferin' little barrel of a chap from the mainland and what do *you* do? You go swaggerin' off like you always do and come back lookin' like a half-opened sardine tin! (*He sits.*) Frankly, Black'eart, I'm disappointed.

BLACKHEART: All right, if you feel so inclined, *you* 'ave a go at 'im. An' I'll lay a five-pun' note to one of your rotten cigars, you never even touch 'im!

BOLLIGREW: Now, now, Black'eart, it's no good carryin' on like that. We've got to think.

BLACKHEART (*dubious*): Think?

BOLLIGREW: That's it; because I'll tell you what, Black'eart; this chap's some sort of disguised intellectual.

BLACKHEART: Oh Lor' . . .

BOLLIGREW: Yes, we're in trouble. Because it's no good pretendin' that you and me are brainy blokes, Blackheart. We're not. You especially . . . (*he rises, he thinks.*) Got it! (*To* STORYTELLER.) You: fetch me Secretary.

STORYTELLER: My lord.

BOLLIGREW: We need help, Blackheart, and I think I know where we can get it.

Enter SECRETARY

Secretary, take a letter.

SECRETARY *mimes shorthand while* BOLLIGREW *strolls about, dictating.*

To Doctor Beelzebub Moloch, Dean of the Faculty of Magic and Regius Professor of Wickedness, at the University, Oxford. 'My dear Moloch, finding myself in a difficulty, my thoughts turn to the most distinguished living practitioner of the Art of Magic.' No, say 'the Science of Magic'. He'll like that. 'The situation is one which I know will engage your disinterested attention, but I need hardly say that expense is no object.' No, that's a bit crude . . . 'disinterested attention but I shall of course expect to defray your expenses.' Er, 'perhaps you could spare me a week or two of your valuable time during the next long vac., Yours etc. Bolligrew.'

Enter STORYTELLER, *looking grave.*

STORYTELLER: Baron Bolligrew, there is a letter for *you*.

BOLLIGREW: Oh?

STORYTELLER: It's from the Dragon.

   All flinch.

BLACKHEART (*rising*): The *Dragon?*

SECRETARY: D-dragon!

BOLLIGREW: How d'you know it's from the Dragon?

STORYTELLER: I know the handwriting, my lord. And – it's in an asbestos envelope.

BOLLIGREW (*licking his lips*): Well, bring it.

   Exit STORYTELLER.

BLACKHEART (*uneasy*): Look here, Bolligrew—

BOLLIGREW (*excited though fearful*): No, wait a bit. This may be very handy.

   Enter STORYTELLER. *He carries in a pair of tongs a large grey envelope, which smokes slightly.* BOLLIGREW *takes it, gingerly opens it.*

   A magnesium flash and smoke rises from envelope. BOLLIGREW *blows on his fingers, extracts paper, charred at the edges. The others watch as he reads:*

BOLLIGREW: Ah – ha ...! Eh? ... *What?* (*To* SECRETARY.) You get that letter off to Moloch.

BLACKHEART: What does he say?

BOLLIGREW: He says ... He's hungry.

CURTAIN

ACT TWO

Stage dark save for STORYTELLER's spot.

STORYTELLER: When Doctor Moloch, the Professor of Magic, received the Baron's letter, he was at first reluctant to leave his luxurious rooms in the heart of an ancient University Town for so remote and uncultivated a spot as the Bolligrew Islands. But then he reflected that it would make a change from his usual routine and that the Baron, after all, was rich and could be made to pay.

Lights up. Enter BOLLIGREW, MOLOCH, BLACKHEART.

BOLLIGREW: Enjoy your meal, I hope, Doctor?

MOLOCH: Passable. Bolligrew, on the first of the month I must be back on the mainland. I am to address an important meeting of the Merlin Society. Let's get down to business.

BOLLIGREW: Right. Well first there's this Royal Knight Errant, Oblong.

MOLOCH: Yes. You wish him made away with? Turned into a frog – something of that order?

BOLLIGREW: No! If he disappears altogether we shall have trouble from the mainland; Duke; King, maybe.

MOLOCH: Awkward. And then?

BOLLIGREW: Then there's the Dragon.

MOLOCH: Yes. This is an aspect of your matter which I don't much care for, Bolligrew. Tell me again?

BOLLIGREW: Well as you know, we 'ave this agreement. I 'ave this side of the island for grindin' the faces of the poor, and Dragon 'as that side of the Island for ravagin'.

MOLOCH: And now he says?

BOLLIGREW: Now 'e says 'e's ravaged it! There's nothin' more to eat there, and he's hungry.

MOLOCH: Hungry. I like it less and less, you know. And in his letter he proposes—?

BOLLIGREW: He proposes I should let him have half *my* half. Well I can see as far through a brick wall as the next chap. Thin end of the wedge, that is.

MOLOCH: Mmm . . . You do realize, Bolligrew, that a spell against a Dragon would be expensive?

BOLLIGREW: Oh yes.

MOLOCH: I mean really very expensive.

BOLLIGREW: Bound to be. Not far short of ten quid, I was thinkin'.

MOLOCH (*amused*): Ten pounds? Twenty-five. Guineas.

BOLLIGREW: . . . All right. Done.

They shake hands. MOLOCH *paces away considering.*

BLACKHEART: Tricky situation, eh?

MOLOCH (*patronizing smile*): I dare say we shall think of something, Squire. This Oblong – Unselfish? Gentle? High principles? Nice with the kiddies? Kind to animals? In short, a *good* man?

BLACKHEART: Sickenin'. He talks to animals.

MOLOCH: And they understand him?

BOLLIGREW: Seem to.

MOLOCH: Then he's very good. Unless like me he's very bad.

Which isn't very likely. Excellent. Dragons like good men.

BLACKHEART: Do they?

MOLOCH: Yes, they have a flavour all of their own . . . Gentlemen, if the Dragon were to eat Sir Oblong, this would dispose of Sir Oblong – pretty finally – and I don't think we need anticipate any very fevered reaction from the mainland. For a Knight Errant to be eaten is an occupational risk and common enough.

BLACKHEART: Right!

MOLOCH: If Sir Oblong had previously been treated with some reliable dragon poison . . . well that would dispose of the Dragon, would it not?

BLACKHEART: I must say, Moloch, when you clever fellers put on your thinkin' caps – it's a treat to listen to yer.

MOLOCH: Thank you Squire. It remains to effect a meeting between the Dragon and our victim.

BOLLIGREW: Yes it does! 'Cause I tell you Moloch, if once that beast sets foot in my half of the island—!

MOLOCH: No no, the victim will go to him. Either you as my client, or I as your consultant, will say 'Oblong, at such an hour on such a day, be off to the Dragon's den', and off he will go.

BLACKHEART: Will he? Why?

MOLOCH: Because, my dear Squire, he will be under a spell; another rather expensive spell I'm afraid, Baron, the ingredients are very costly, very rare – snake's feet, fish feathers things of that sort – shall we say another twenty-five?

BOLLIGREW: Another twent—! That's fifty quid!

MOLOCH: Guineas. Bolligrew, in mine as any other profession, cheap is cheap – and your Dragon is no fool.

BLACKHEART: Somethin' in that you know.

BOLLIGREW (*venomous*): . . . All right. Agreed.

MOLOCH: Very wise. (*To* STORYTELLER.) I shall need a small basket of apples.

STORYTELLER: I have them here, Doctor.

Produces them from wings.

MOLOCH: These will do nicely. And now I need Sir Oblong.

STORYTELLER (*gravely*): Yes Doctor, I know. (*Going, turns.*) Doctor—

MOLOCH: Well?

STORYTELLER: Are you sure you want this?

MOLOCH: You are I think the Storyteller?

STORYTELLER: Yes.

MOLOCH: Then you know what's going to happen in the story?

STORYTELLER: Yes, that's why I—

MOLOCH (*holds up hand*): You're certain you know what's going to happen.

STORYTELLER: Quite certain.

MOLOCH: That must give you a pleasant feeling of superiority. However, if you're quite certain you know what will happen, whatever it is will happen quite certainly.

STORYTELLER: Yes.

MOLOCH (*shrill*): Then what is the good of asking me if I *want* it to happen? . . . Like everyone else, so far as I'm able, I'll *do* what I want.

STORYTELLER: Just so, Doctor.

MOLOCH: Then, Sir Oblong?

Exit STORYTELLER.

The path to Hell is paved with good intentions. It must be very soggy underfoot.

Turns briskly and calls.

MOLOCH: Mazeppa!

Enter behind the others, MAZEPPA, *a magpie, carrying box and books.*

BLACKHEART: Eh!

BOLLIGREW: Magpie!

He raises gun. But MOLOCH *stamps foot and points an imperious finger; magnesium flash, gun flies from* BOLLIGREW's *hand, himself shaking as from electric shock.*

Wh-wh-wh-wa-wa-what the bl-up-lu-blazes—

MOLOCH (*indifferently*): Mazeppa my dear, prepare the ground for the mortification of apples while I look up the incantation.

MAZEPPA takes chalk from box and draws complex caballistic pattern on floor, while MOLOCH *consults book.*

MOLOCH: You have had a narrow escape, Bolligrew, Mazeppa is my familiar. The bird is priceless and took years to train. Had you shot him I should probably have lost my temper and done something irreversible to you. Yes, here we are. Is all ready, Mazeppa?

MAZEPPA: Ready, Master.

Hands wand to MOLOCH, *receiving from him the book from which he reads in a low croaking monotone, circling round the pattern in which the apple is placed.*

Bumbly-wumbly, peejly-weejly. Weejly-peejly bumbly wumbly, etc. . . .

MOLOCH (*over* MAZEPPA *and much clearer*):

That Oblong with his own last breath
May be the means of Dragon's death,
Lord of Darkness hear the plea
Of Beelzebub Moloch, P.H.D. !

Rosy apple, healthy fruit
Of healthy tree with healthy root,
I call down by magic art
The unqualified canker of the heart.

I summon up my utmost might
And plant in you the invisible blight.
That he who tastes may wish for more
Taste sweet and sound, AND HAVE NO CORE!

Thin column of smoke rises from apple, as MOLOCH *applies wand to it.*

Splendid. Clean up Mazeppa and make the usual entry in the journal.

The others come cautiously forward and peer warily at the apple.

It's quite safe gentlemen; what you saw was merely the virtue leaving it. *But* – any person who eats so much as one bite of this apple, becomes instant Dragon poison.

BLACKHEART: Well I call that dashed ingenious.

Exit MAZEPPA *with props.*

MOLOCH: A simple process, Squire, but effective. Our next task is more difficult. In order to bring Oblong in our power, I need from him some dearly prized possession.

BLACKHEART: Oblong's got no prized possessions.

BOLLIGREW: Yes 'e 'as. That purple mantle!

BLACKHEART *(touched on the raw evidently)*: Ah!

MOLOCH: He prizes it?

BLACKHEART *(resentful)*: 'E prizes it all right. Swaggerin' up an' down the 'Igh Street . . .

BOLLIGREW: Never takes it off!

MOLOCH: We must persuade him to.

BLACKHEART (*looking off*): 'E's 'ere.

MOLOCH: I must have that mantle.

   Enter OBLONG.

OBLONG: Good evening, Baron.

BOLLIGREW: 'Evening, Oblong! What brings you up here?

OBLONG: I have a serious complaint to make.

BOLLIGREW: Oh?

   Listens attentively to OBLONG, *motioning* BLACKHEART
   to come behind and clumsily attempt to detach mantle.

OBLONG: Obidiah Bobblenob has been placed in the stocks
   on the village green.

BOLLIGREW: Has he?

OBLONG: He has. And your men-at-arms are pelting him with
   treacle pies. Hot, treacle pies.

BOLLIGREW: Are they now?

OBLONG: They are, as I expect you know — (*Spins, draws
   sword.*) Blackheart, what are you about?

MOLOCH (*hastily coming forward, benign, ecclesiastical*): Is it
   Oblong *Fitz* Oblong?

OBLONG: Er, well, yes.

MOLOCH: Let me take your hand sir. In these degenerate
   days, a real Knight Errant of the good old school – a privilege.
   My name is Innocent, Doctor Innocent, Dean of Divinity
   and unworthy Professor of Goodness at the University.

OBLONG (*respectfully*): Oh. A privilege to meet *you* sir.

MOLOCH: Er . . . (*draws him aside.*) You're having a wonderful
   effect here you know.

OBLONG: Things are a little better than they were I suppose.

MOLOCH: Wonderfully better, wonderfully. And you know
   (*very confidential*) you're beginning to have an effect on our
   friend here.

OBLONG: Bolligrew?

MOLOCH: I know. But I have been poor Jasper's spiritual adviser many years now – stony ground, Sir Oblong, stony ground – but there's good in the man, oh yes. And *you*, have set it in motion, where I failed.

OBLONG: Well I should like to think so—

MOLOCH: My son—

BOLLIGREW: Er, yes, Father?

MOLOCH: I want you to go and release that poor fellow from the stocks.

BOLLIGREW: Oh. Er, very well, Father. (*Going.*)

MOLOCH: And humbly beg his pardon.

BOLLIGREW: Eh?

MOLOCH: As an act of repentance. You will feel the better for it, won't he, Sir Oblong? (*Behind* OBLONG's *back nodding vigorously at* BOLLIGREW.)

OBLONG: You will, Bolligrew, honestly.

BOLLIGREW: Oh. Well. If *you* say so, Oblong . . . (*To* BLACKHEART.) Comn' repentin' then?

Exit with BLACKHEART.

OBLONG: I must say that's very gratifying.

MOLOCH: A great gift of yours, this, Sir Oblong. Mightier than the sword I do assure you.

OBLONG: Doctor, you make me ashamed.

MOLOCH: No no. Yours is a noble calling. Ah this is the famous purple mantle. A prized possession I imagine.

OBLONG: I must confess it is.

MOLOCH: And rightly so. Dear, dear, it's torn.

OBLONG: It's a hurly-burly sort of life, Doctor.

MOLOCH: Let me repair it. (*Trying to take it.*)

OBLONG: Oh no – (*alarmed*) – really—

MOLOCH (*desists with a silvery chuckle*): The workman is worthy of his hire. I was at one time, Abbot of St Clare's and there our daily task was the repair and manufacture of – oh church vestments, altar cloths, exquisite work; I often regret those quiet days with the needle. (*Unfastens mantle.*) And you will give much pleasure to a foolish old man in the evening of his days.

OBLONG: But I never – (*falters under* MOLOCH's *gentle gaze*) – never take it off – really . . .

MOLOCH (*wags a roguish finger*): Never take it off Sir Oblong? Do I detect a little vanity at work? A last little flicker of worldly pride?

OBLONG (*relinquishes it*): I shall value it the more for your attention.

MOLOCH: Well . . .! Oh – before I go, sir, let me press you to an apple. I always bring a basket for Jasper. I grow them myself in the college garden. Do tell me what you think.

Hands OBLONG *the enchanted apple.* OBLONG *bites.*

MOLOCH: Good?

OBLONG: It's perfect!

MOLOCH: Well, you if anyone should know perfection – even in an apple.

OBLONG (*delighted – deprecating*): Oh, Doctor—

MOLOCH: No false modesty I beg. (*Going, turns.*) Let Oblong put his faith in Oblong's goodness, and Oblong is invincible.

Exit MOLOCH. *Enter* STORYTELLER.

OBLONG: That excellent old man came just in time!

STORYTELLER: Indeed?

OBLONG: Indeed. I was in danger of adopting violent and even underhand methods on this mission.

STORYTELLER: And now?

OBLONG: Now I shall rely on simple goodness.

STORYTELLER: I see. Is that wise?

OBLONG: Wise? It's right! Oh how much better to have reformed Bolligrew than merely to have conquered him.

STORYTELLER: Have you reformed Bolligrew?

OBLONG: I've made a start. (*Beaming, excited, complacent.*) It seems I have a gift for it.

STORYTELLER: And will you reform – the Dragon?

OBLONG: The Dragon . . . ! I say that *would* be something . . . after all I reformed Michael Magpie.

STORYTELLER: Did you now?

OBLONG: Oh yes – he used to be a thief you know—

STORYTELLER: Used to be?

> Enter MAGPIE *running. Skids to a halt when he sees them. We see behind his back the twinkling Lord Mayor's Chain.*

MAGPIE: Ark!

OBLONG (*pleased*): Ah – Michael – we were just— (*Notices* MAGPIE's *awkwardly innocent posture.*) Michael?

MAGPIE: Ark?

OBLONG: What have you got behind your back?

MAGPIE: Behind my back?

> *Elaborately searches stage behind him, passing chain from hand to hand to keep it hidden as he turns.*

OBLONG: Michael!

MAGPIE: Ark . . (*Shows chain.*)

> STORYTELLER *coughs discreetly, looks dryly at* OBLONG.

STORYTELLER: *Now*, what will you do? (*Adds quickly.*) Think, Sir Oblong.

OBLONG: Think? What is there to think about? Degenerate bird!

MAGPIE: I'm sorry Obby. 'E left it in the garden you see, and the sun was shinin' and it twinkled . . .

OBLONG: That was the temptation. Did you resist? You did not. It twinkled, so you took it – and there we have you in a nutshell.

MAGPIE: Ark.

OBLONG: You may well say so. (*Takes chain.*) I am only thankful Dr Innocent has not witnessed this.

MAGPIE: Ark! Well if you ask me – there's something very fishy about that old geyser—

OBLONG: So! Not content with telling untruths, with breaking your word, with thieving – you would now plant in my mind contemptible suspicions against a fine old gentleman who was once the Abbot of St Clare's!

STORYTELLER *makes gesture of helplessness and exits.*

Michael, it pains me to say this because there is something about you, a certain – gaiety . . . high spirits . . . which has won my affection.

MAGPIE (*bending neck to* OBLONG's *caress. Softly*): Ark . . .

OBLONG (*sharply removing hand*): But that is superficial! You are an unworthy instrument Michael, and until my mission is accomplished, I may not regard you as my friend.

Exit OBLONG.

MAGPIE (*stricken*): Ark! Obby—? I won't do it again . . .! (*Silence. He sniffs.*) Well *I* don't care. See if I do. (*Hops about stage, jaunty and forlorn, improvising.*)

Hi diddledidee,
A Magpie's life for me,
I pinched the Lord Mayor's Chain . . .
An I 'spect I'll do it again . . .

I'm happy and I'm free—

A Magpie's life . . . (*Voice tails, unhappily.*)

Oh dash it! Obby? (*He stumps off, saying tearful and aggrieved*) It *twinkled* . . .! I *like* twinkly things . . .! *I* can't help it . . .!

Exit MAGPIE. *Before his exit is complete, enter opposite* MAZEPPA, MOLOCH, BLACKHEART, BOLLIGREW. *Lights dim. Their air is tense, they keep their voices low. Stop. All look to* MOLOCH.

MOLOCH: Twilight. I can now perform the spell to make one person subject to another. The screen, Mazeppa.

MAZEPPA *erects screen and carries box inside, while* MOLOCH *stands tense and listening.*

BOLLIGREW: Er, Moloch—

MOLOCH: Sh—!

BOLLIGREW: What?

MOLOCH: I want to hear an owl cry and a church clock strike the hour. (*Instantly, distant bell chimes, and an owl shrieks nearby.*) Excellent. Prized possession, Bolligrew. (*Goes towards screen.*)

BOLLIGREW: Moloch, I want to watch this.

MOLOCH: Watch? This is Grimbleboots, probably the most powerful spell in the civilized world – it is certainly the most secret.

BOLLIGREW: I want to watch.

MOLOCH: Out of the question.

BOLLIGREW: In that case, Moloch, I'll ask you for a little demonstration.

MOLOCH: Demonstration?

BOLLIGREW: That's it. Pop this in with the other prized possession, will you?

Produces BLACKHEART's *black plume from under jacket,
and gives it to* MOLOCH, *sweetly.*

Just to make sure I'm gettin' me money's worth, you know.

MOLOCH: Bolligrew, I find you offensive.

BOLLIGREW: Aye, most chaps do.

    MOLOCH *behind screen;* BLACKHEART *turns.*

BLACKHEART: 'Ave they started?

BOLLIGREW: Just goin' to.

    Together they regard the screen.

BLACKHEART (*wistful*): I envy these brainy blokes, Bolligrew.
Must make life deuced interestin'.

    BOLLIGREW *unsympathetic grunt.*

MOLOCH: Quiet, please gentlemen!

    *Short pause. Then in the dispassionate manner of surgeons,
aeroplane pilots or other practised technicians.*

Retort?

MAZEPPA: Retort.

MOLOCH: Burner?

MAZEPPA: Burner.

MOLOCH: Essay.

    Thin column of illuminated pink smoke rises. MOLOCH *and*
MAZEPPA, *overlapping as before.*

Trim-spickle-tickle, trim-spickle-tickle, trim-spickle-tickle,
trim-spickle-tickle, trim-spickly-wickly . . . Grimbleboots!

MAZEPPA: – Grimbleboots.

MOLOCH: Portent?

MAZEPPA: Portent.

MOLOCH: Presto!

    *A soft explosion and billowing cloud of blue smoke, brightly lit.
Twangings and bashings of cymbals and harps on Speaker.*

BLACKHEART: Fascinatin'.

BOLLIGREW: Yes. Needs to be, for fifty quid.

MOLOCH: Prognostication?

MAZEPPA: Possible.

MOLOCH: Proceed.

Accompanied by more effects on Speaker, overlapping.

Scrambled-shambles, pickled-winkles, frightening-lightning, eevil-weevil, Knight's a nuisance, Knight's a mess; what he has is his alone and won't be Bolligrew's *unless*—

MAZEPPA: – won't be *Bolligrew's unless*—

BLACKHEART (*nudging* BOLLIGREW): 'Mentioned you then, old man.

BOLLIGREW: Shut up.

MOLOCH (*rising excitement*): Shamble's scrambled—

MAZEPPA (*rising excitement*): Winkle's pickled—

MOLOCH: Lightning frightens—

MAZEPPA: Weevil's evil—

BOTH: By powers of unhappiness!

MAZEPPA (*cries out*): Misery!

MOLOCH (*cries out*): Poverty!

MAZEPPA: Woe!

MOLOCH (*screams*): Precipitation!

Frantic twangings and bashings on Speaker, a geyser of sparks, coloured balls, magnesium streamers, cloud of smoke. MOLOCH *emerges with mantle.*

BLACKHEART: First class show, Doctor. Never seen anythin' like it! Can I 'ave a squint be'ind the scenes?

MOLOCH: By all means, Squire.

BLACKHEART *goes behind screen.* MOLOCH *hands mantle and plume to* BOLLIGREW.

BOLLIGREW: Don't look any different to me, Moloch.

MOLOCH: I should hope not indeed. The prized possession must be returned to its owner. Only if he accepts it is he in your power.

BOLLIGREW: Oh. (*Calls.*) Blackheart!

BLACKHEART (*emerging*): Terrible smell in there. Yes, old man? Me plume! Where d'you get it?

BOLLIGREW: Oh, feller picked it up somewhere. D'you want it?

BLACKHEART: I should say. (*Jamming it into socket of helmet.*) Felt 'alf naked without me plume.

MOLOCH: He is in our power. Squire—

BLACKHEART: Yes?

MOLOCH: Sit-down!

 BLACKHEART *collapses instantly. Startled, then agreeably.*

BLACKHEART: Like that?

MOLOCH: Get up.

 BLACKHEART *levitates.*

 Can you dance?

BLACKHEART: Dance? Lor' no—

MOLOCH: Try.

 Minuet on Speaker; BLACKHEART *dances.* BOLLIGREW *enchanted.*

BOLLIGREW: 'Ere – 'ere – let me 'ave a go – Black'eart!

 BLACKHEART *stops.*

BLACKHEART: Yes old man?

 BOLLIGREW *struggles with the wealth of possibility. A moment of inspiration.*

BOLLIGREW: Be a teapot!

 BLACKHEART *stands on one leg, one arm cranked forward as the spout, the other crooked behind him as the handle.*

MOLOCH: Enough, Baron?

BOLLIGREW (*smile fades*): Not quite, Moloch. **Blackheart.** (*He points.*) Off to the Dragon's den.

BLACKHEART: Dragon's den, old man?

BOLLIGREW: That's right, old man.

BLACKHEART: Oh. All right. (*Goes clanking off-stage, false exit.*)

BOLLIGREW: 'E's goin'!

MOLOCH: Yes, you'd better stop him.

BOLLIGREW: Blackheart!

BLACKHEART *re-enters.*

BLACKHEART: Yes old man?

BOLLIGREW: 'Ang on. (*To* MOLOCH *delighted.*) 'E does it all quite willing, don't 'e?

MOLOCH: Oh the victim does not know he is a victim. A small refinement of my own. Tell him to remove the prized possession.

BOLLIGREW: Take your plume off.

BLACKHEART *takes off plume, shudders and 'comes to'. Magic effect on Speaker.*

BLACKHEART: Well if you ask me, Bolligrew that was in dashed poor taste!

MOLOCH: Mazeppa, take the Squire's plume and burn it. And Mazeppa, kindly make your entry in the journal with more care. The one for this morning is barely legible.

MAZEPPA: Yes, Master.

Exit MAZEPPA *with props.*

MOLOCH: Now let's see where we are: Oblong has eaten the apple – which makes him dragon poison. You have the prized possession – which gives you power to send him *to* the dragon. It remains to enquire of the Dragon when he would like to dine.

BOLLIGREW: Aye. Right.

BLACKHEART: Er. You goin' to the Dragon's den, old man?

BOLLIGREW: That's right, Black'eart an' you're comin' with me.

BLACKHEART: Oh. When?

BOLLIGREW: Now.

They turn backs to audience and freeze as lights dim further and STORYTELLER *enters.*

STORYTELLER: The Dragon lived in a black and silent valley which had once been green with pasture. His den looked like a railway tunnel without any signals or track.

Black backdrop descends to cover church, with black archway in it.

Those who had seen him, by moonlight, knew that he was bigger than four carthorses, and sleek, and black, and shiny. Like all black dragons he seldom came out except at night, because his eyes were weak. And in the day, these eyes were all that could be seen of him.

Red eyes switched on in blackness of arch.

And all that could be heard of him was an occasional roar—

DRAGON *roars on Speaker.*

And an occasional complaint; for the Dragon was always discontented, and talked to himself continually.

DRAGON (*on Speaker throughout*): 'I'm bored . . . There's no avoiding it; I'm thoroughly bored. . . .'

BLACKHEART: Look 'ere, Bolligrew. You see I've just remembered a pressin' engagement.

BOLLIGREW: Well forget it again.

He draws the upstage towards the tunnel. Exit STORYTELLER *simultaneously.*

Hello . . .? Afternoon . . .! Anyone at 'ome?

DRAGON: 'Do I hear the voice of a human bean?'

On Speaker, noise between that of approaching train and cantering horse; eyes growing larger.

BOLLIGREW: It's me! Bolligrew!

Clatter of hooves, squeal of brakes. Hiss. Smoke curls from tunnel roof.

DRAGON: 'Oh . . . Bolligrew . . . Is that Moloch?'

BOLLIGREW: Dragon, we're a bit pressed for time. This proposal of yours for takin' over half of my half of the Island—

DRAGON: – 'Yes?'

BOLLIGREW: Seems quite reasonable to me.

DRAGON: 'It does? . . . That's odd . . . Baron, there are no *strings* attached to this, are there?'

BOLLIGREW (*reels out of* DRAGON's *sight, mopping brow with handkerchief. Shakily*): Strings, old chap? Don't know what you mean!

DRAGON: 'Moloch. *You* haven't anything up your smelly old sleeve, have you?'

MOLOCH: A reasonable suspicion, Dragon, but the answer happens to be 'no'. There's something we want you to do.

DRAGON: 'That's better. What?'

BOLLIGREW: Well it's about this feller Oblong. I don't know if you've heard—

DRAGON: 'I have heard, yes.'

BOLLIGREW: Well we were wonderin', if he 'appened to come wanderin' over 'ere, if you might like to, er, well – nosh 'im!

DRAGON: 'But Baron, people *don't* wander over here.'

MOLOCH: He will dragon, he will. We are using Grimbleboots. He will come very quietly – if you wish it, *without* his sword.

DRAGON: Understand. Is he a good man?

MOLOCH: All the way through I think. I shall be interested to hear.

DRAGON: Well. That's worth waiting for.

MOLOCH: Tomorrow then, at three o'clock?

DRAGON: Tomorrow at three.

BOLLIGREW: There we are then! Good-bye old chap!

DRAGON: 'Good-bye Baron, good-bye. . . .'

Eye-lights off. Backcloth flies revealing Church. MOLOCH, BOLLIGREW, BLACKHEART *freeze until enter* OBLONG.

MOLOCH: Ah there you are, sir. We have been all over the Island looking for you. Here's your mended mantle.

OBLONG: Oh thank you. Doctor.

MOLOCH: Turn around sir, and I'll put it on.

OBLONG *does so, but just before* MOLOCH *can clip it on his back he moves away and turns.*

OBLONG: I wonder if I should? You're right you know – it's only vanity and worldly pride.

Consternation among the conspirators. MOLOCH *recovers.*

MOLOCH: Come sir, don't be solemn. I spoke in jest!

OBLONG: Oh. (*An uneasy laugh. Returns, and* MOLOCH *tries again. Again* OBLONG *moves away.*) Many true words spoken in jest, Doctor.

MOLOCH (*rather severe*): I shall begin to think so. Did Gallahad refuse his suit of snow white armour?

BOLLIGREW: Yes.

MOLOCH: No. But Oblong will affect to be unworthy of his purple robe. Here's vanity indeed.

OBLONG: Oh. (*The same again. Moves away again.*) As a gesture of humility you mean.

MOLOCH: Precisely.

OBLONG *nods, is put into the mantle. Is struck by their sudden tension.*

OBLONG: Gentlemen?

BOLLIGREW: 'Ow d'you feel?

OBLONG (*puzzled*): Thank you Baron, the best of health. . . .

MOLOCH(*points*): Oblong. Sit down.

OBLONG *sits.*

BLACKHEART: Stand up.

OBLONG *obeys.*

BOLLIGREW: On your knees.

OBLONG *obeys. They loom over him.*

BOLLIGREW: Well now, you are going to be my guest at the castle for a day.

OBLONG: Oh, thank you.

BOLLIGREW: Don't mention it. At three o'clock tomorrow you are going to the Dragon's Den.

OBLONG(*pleasantly*): The Dragon's Den?

MOLOCH: Just a social call you know.

BOLLIGREW: So leave your sword outside.

OBLONG: My sword? (*Seems to struggle for a moment then*) Whatever you say, Baron.

BOLLIGREW: That's it *exactly* – whatever I say. Stand up. Now cut down to the castle, introduce yourself to the butler, an' 'e'll show you straight to your dungeon.

OBLONG: Then I'll say au revoir.

BOLLIGREW: You say that.

OBLONG: Au revoir.

Exit OBLONG, BLACKHEART *and* BOLLIGREW *watch him, off, fascinated.*

BLACKHEART: 'E 'asn't a clue, 'as 'e?

BOLLIGREW: Not a blazin' clue! (*Turns.*) An' will he go

off, just like that, to the Dragon's Den?

MOLOCH: At three o'clock tomorrow, just like that; no power on earth can stop him!

BOLLIGREW, MOLOCH, BLACKHEART, *exit. Enter* STORY-TELLER.

STORYTELLER: Now, while all this was happening on the Island, back on the mainland the Duke and his Knights in armour—

Breaks off as enter KNIGHTS *and* DUKE, *trundling Round Table, crossing others who push off Church. All sit and freeze.*

– The Knights in armour were finding that the programme outlined by the Duke, and which they had so much looked forward to, was less enjoyable than they had thought.

DUKE (*heavily*): Anything on the agenda, Juniper?

JUNIPER: The menu for Your Grace's birthday party; er, meringues, raspberry jelly, pickled shrimps, ginger snaps and lemonade.

Murmur of boredom and discontent. Snappish.

If any of you gentlemen can think of something better—!

DUKE: No. No. That will do as well as anything . . . I suppose. (*Looking round.*) Any other business?

TRUMPINGTON: There's a *rumour* going round that there's a dragon;

On 'Dragon', stir of interest all round.

– down Little Gidding way.

STRONGBODY: I've seen it, gentlemen. 'T's not a dragon. 'T's a big lizard.

All slump again.

SMOOTHE: Anyone know anything about this damsel in distress at East Coker?

Stir of interest again.

1ST KNIGHT: Went over yesterday, gentlemen. No more distressed than I am.

All slump again.

Deucedly plain girl she was, too . . .

JUNIPER: Well (*sighs*) that seems to be all, then. (*Shuts minute book.*) Musical bumps?

DUKE: Might as well.

Music on Speaker. KNIGHTS *and* DUKE *tramp gloomily round stage in circle. Each time the music stops* KNIGHTS *careful to allow* DUKE *to seat himself first, then compete among themselves.* DUKE *calls out the losers.*

Trumpington . . . ! Dashwood . . . ! Graceless . . . !

Etc. until only DUKE *and* SMOOTHE *left. Music stops,* SMOOTHE *assists* DUKE *to floor, where he remains, gloomily.*

You're out Smoothe.

SMOOTHE returns to table. Flutter of half-hearted applause from KNIGHTS.

DUKE: What's the prize?

SMOOTHE (*bringing it*): Chocolates, your Grace.

Returns, sits. DUKE, *still on floor.*

DUKE: 'Don't know how it is, gentlemen . . . Musical bumps— Hasn't got the same excitement, somehow . . . Nor chocolates.

1ST KNIGHT: Not like it was in Oblong's day.

STRONGBODY: Ah.

TRUMPINGTON: Always plenty goin' on then.

1ST KNIGHT: One thing after another.

JUNIPER: Best man we ever had.

1ST KNIGHT: First class.

SMOOTHE (*uncomfortable*): Oh, capital.

DUKE (*from floor*): That was a dirty trick you played on Oblong. Smoothe.

SMOOTHE: Well, really!

DUKE: You thought of it.

1ST KNIGHT: Wonder how he's gettin' on there.

STRONGBODY (*envious*): Up to his neck in it, I bet.

1ST KNIGHT: Deuced if I don't go and see!

TRUMPINGTON: Make a change.

SMOOTHE: – It would.

STRONGBODY: Hanged if I don't come with you!

SMOOTHE: So will I!

TRUMPINGTON: – Me too!

JUNIPER: – And me!

Excited babble; all sitting forward. DUKE *follows all this jealously and now rises.*

DUKE: Gentlemen!

Silence.

An excellent suggestion, but there won't be cabin-space for more than two – and *I* have had in mind for some time now to pay a State Visit to the Bolligrew Islands.

1ST KNIGHT (*sotto*): Well, really . . .!

SMOOTHE (*smoothly*): I remember Your Grace mentioned that to me the other day.

DUKE (*surprised*): Did I? Yes I believe I did. Smoothe, you can come with me.

SMOOTHE: Very civil of you, sir.

DUKE: I think that's all gentlemen. Meeting adjourned.

1ST KNIGHT: Well I'll be jiggered.

Exit KNIGHTS *with Round Table.* DUKE *addresses* STORY-TELLER.

DUKE: Would you have my galleon got ready please?

STORYTELLER: It's ready now Your Grace.

Enter CAPTAIN *as before, but now his sail is purple.*

DUKE (*nervously*): If you could arrange for the weather to be better than it usually is . . .?

STORYTELLER: It's always the same for *that* voyage, Your Grace.

DUKE: No matter. It's not my way to be deflected from the path of duty by a little wind and rain.

STORYTELLER: No Your Grace.

DUKE '*Boards*' *galleon, assisted by* SMOOTHE *who enters with umbrella which he opens as thunder and lightning crash and boat moves. Enter opposite,* BOLLIGREW *and* BLACKHEART.

BOLLIGREW: Well Black'eart, today's the day – at three o'clock this afternoon our troubles will be ov—

Thunder and lightning. DUKE *seasick upstage, presenting posterior,* SMOOTHE *solicitous.*

'Ello? Must be someone comin'!

BLACKHEART *scans* DUKE *through telescope.*

BLACKHEART: Oh yes. Must be somebody important.

BOLLIGREW: Oh?

BLACKHEART: Purple sails.

BOLLIGREW: Purp—?

Snatches telescope.

Ber-lazes . . .! It's the Duke!

BLACKHEART: 'Oo?

BOLLIGREW: The Duke! I'd know that face anywhere.

BLACKHEART: Ah. Duke, eh?

BOLLIGREW: Yes! 'E's comin' to see Oblong!

BLACKHEART (*nodding sagely*): Very likely.

BOLLIGREW: So 'ow can we feed Oblong to the dragon?

BLACKHEART: Oh. We can't then.

BOLLIGREW: That's right, Blackheart we can't. And what's Dragon goin' to do if we don't? I'll tell you what 'e's goin' to do Blackheart – 'e's goin' to ravage – indiscriminate! Whackin' great black dragon, ragin' up an' down the 'Igh Street like as not, roarin' for 'is nosh – as promised 'im, Blackheart by you an' me – 'an that's goin' to take a bit of explainin' too, isn't it?

BLACKHEART: Well what are we goin' to do then?

BOLLIGREW: *I* don't know . . .! (*Mumbles to himself.*) What are we goin' to do . . .? (*Roars at audience.*) What are we – goin' – to— (*Breaks off as he sees* STORYTELLER.) 'Ere, you, what do we do?

STORYTELLER: You consult Dr Moloch.

BOLLIGREW: Moloch!

BLACKHEART: Moloch!

BOLLIGREW (*calls*): Moloch!

Enter behind him MOLOCH.

MOLOCH: Yes?

BOLLIGREW: Look.

MOLOCH *scans* DUKE, *as* DUKE, SMOOTHE, CAPTAIN *exit.*

MOLOCH: Dear, dear. This is an unexpected complication.

BOLLIGREW: Unexpected comp—? It's a blazin' disaster!

MOLOCH: On the contrary, a golden opportunity.

BOLLIGREW: You thought of somethin'?

MOLOCH: I have thought of a way whereby we can send Oblong to the Dragon, and send the Duke away well satisfied with matters here. I should not be surprised if he conferred a Knighthood on the Squire, and on yourself, the order of the golden artichoke.

BOLLIGREW
BLACKHEART } (*advancing, fascinated*): Eh? What? 'Ow?

MOLOCH: You wish a consultation?

BOLLIGREW: 'Ow much?

MOLOCH: My consultation fee is fifteen guineas.

BOLLIGREW: Make it quids.

MOLOCH: Guineas. The Duke will be here in half an hour.

BOLLIGREW: All right – guineas!

MOLOCH: Then listen to my plot . . .

They join him, put heads together, conspiratorial, backs to audience.

STORYTELLER: It was a very wicked plan which Doctor Moloch outlined—

They all glance round baleful and suspicious at audience, then huddle again.

As you shall shortly see.

They break up, guffawing.

MOLOCH: So Baron, if I can handle Oblong, can you handle the Duke?

BOLLIGREW: Leave that to me – I know these bigwigs. Corporal!

Enter CORPORAL *running.*

CORPORAL: Me lord?

BOLLIGREW: Duke's comin'. Turn out the population. Everyone wearin' 'is best clothes, Corporal – don't want no ostentatious poverty you understand.

COPORAL: Yes me lord.

BOLLIGREW: Issue 'em with shoes, an' everyone to 'ave one packet of paper streamers. Right gettit done. Lord Mayor!

Exit CORPORAL, *enter* MAYOR, *running.*

MAYOR: Baron?

BOLLIGREW: 'Got those flags we' ad for the Coronation?

MAYOR: Yes Baron?

BOLLIGREW: Gettem up, Duke's comin'. Cook!

Exit MAYOR, *enter* COOK, *running.*

COOK: My lord?

BOLLIGREW: Duke's comin'. Grade one banquet, twelve o'clock sharp. Orchestra!

Exit COOK, *enter* DRUMMER *and* CYMBALIST *running. Thud and clash.*

Duke's comin'. We'll want the National Anthem an' something' jolly. Tune up.

Musicians tune noisily (Speaker augmenting) while enter PEASANTS *carrying shoes, and* CORPORAL.

CORPORAL: Lef-ri lef-ri lef-ri lef-riiii – Alt! Siddown. Put yer shoes on. Other foot, stupid!

Enter MAYOR, *backing, calling off*:

MAYOR: Lower away then! Lower away! Thank you!

Strings of coloured flags descend.

CORPORAL: On yer feet!

PEASANTS *rise,* CORPORAL *salutes.*

Ready me lord!

MOLOCH: Now then. (*Raises hand.*) Oblong, by the power of Grimbleboots, be here.

Enter OBLONG, *followed unobtrusively by* OBIDIAH *and* MAGPIE.

OBLONG: Good morning, Doctor, Baron. What's all this?

MOLOCH: The Duke has come to see you.

OBLONG: Oh how kind of His Grace!

MOLOCH: Yes. Sir Oblong, when you *meet* the Duke, you are to . . .

OBLONG: I am to what?

MOLOCH: Disgrace yourself.

OBLONG: Disgrace myself? How?

MOLOCH: Well there I thought that you might help me . . .

BOLLIGREW: Pitch a brick through the Lord Mayor's window.

MOLOCH (*hastily*): No no. That's wildly out of character. If you did that His Grace might think that you had been bewitched!

OBLONG (*deprecating chuckle*): Good heavens, that would never do!

MOLOCH: No. Have you ever in *fact* done anything disgraceful?

OBLONG: Oh yes.

MOLOCH: What?

OBLONG: Er . . .

MOLOCH: You haven't, have you?

OBLONG: I do keep myself on a pretty tight rein, I suppose.

MOLOCH: Aha! I knew you'd have the answer! You have kept yourself on a tight rein now for – what? Fifty years?

OBLONG: Thereabouts.

MOLOCH: High time you let yourself go. Oblong, when you meet the Duke you will simply – let yourself go.

OBLONG: But what shall I do if I let myself go?

MOLOCH: You will do all those things which all those years you have wanted to do and have restrained yourself from doing.

OBLONG (*roguish chuckle*): Oh dear . . .

MOLOCH: Yes . . . Off you go then till you're wanted.

OBLONG *going, checks.*

OBLONG: Oh. At three o'clock I have an appointment with the Dragon you know.

MOLOCH: There'll just be nice time. Off with you now. The watchword is: 'Let yourself go'.

BOLLIGREW
MOLOCH   } (*softly in unison*): Let yourself go.
BLACKHEART

OBLONG: Well we *are* going to have an eventful day.

Exit OBLONG, *enter* MAN-AT-ARMS.

MAN-AT-ARMS: Duke's galleon comin' round the 'eadland now me lord!

BOLLIGREW: Right! Duke's comin'! Everybody-y-y – SMILE!

Drum and cymbals strike up. Exit in march step led by BOLLIGREW, *all but* OBIDIAH *and* MAGPIE.

OBIDIAH: What d'you think of that then?

MAGPIE: What do I think? I think – Witchcraft!

Boom of cannon and cheering on Speaker.

STORYTELLER: The cannon fired, the people cheered, and the Duke's private galleon sailed majestically into the harbour. And then for miles around the loyal people of the Island stood smartly to attention as the band struck up – the National Anthem!

'Colonel Bogey' on Speaker. OBIDIAH *and* STORYTELLER *stand rigid.* MAGPIE *idly scratches himself until called to order by* OBIDIAH, *scandalized. More cheering then 'The Lincolnshire Poacher' and grand entrance of* PEASANTS, MEN-AT-ARMS, DUKE, BOLLIGREW, BAND, SMOOTHE, BLACKHEART, MOLOCH *and* MAZEPPA. PEASANTS *prodded by* MEN-AT-ARMS, *cheering and throwing paper streamers over* DUKE *who is enchanted.*

DUKE: Thank you good people! Thank you! Thank you! Well I must say, Bolligrew, I hadn't expected anything like this!

BOLLIGREW: Their own idea Your Grace. I told them Your

Grace wouldn't expect any ceremony, but they would turn
out. Of course Your Grace is very popular in the Islands.

DUKE: Well that's very nice, very nice. I must say Bolligrew,
your people look well cared for.

BOLLIGREW: Now you couldn't 'ave said anythin' which
would give me greater pleasure. That's always been my way:
anythin' for the people. That's a leaf I took out of Your
Grace's book I don't mind admittin'.

DUKE: Well I never. Bolligrew I'm agreeably surprised. I'd
been given to understand that you were a, well rather a
bad Baron?

BOLLIGREW (*sadly*): Ah yes. I've 'eard the tales they tell
about me on the mainland. That church for instance, I dare
say you've been told it was a ruin?

DUKE: I had, yes . . .

BOLLIGREW: Well there it is, there's no stoppin' idle tongues.
Blackheart, I wonder where Oblong is?

DUKE: Yes. I take it somewhat amiss, Smoothe that Oblong
isn't here to meet me.

BOLLIGREW: Oh I think we 'ave to make allowances, Your
Grace. At 'is time of life we must expect a little neglect of
duty. I know Blackheart here has quite a soft spot for the old
reprobate, haven't you?

BLACKHEART: Er. Oh. Yes. Yes, rather. Very fond of 'im, I
am in a way. Bit of a bully, of course, but—

DUKE: Oblong? A bully?

BOLLIGREW: Knocks the peasants about somethin' cruel
sometimes.

LORD MAYOR (*pushing forward, timidly desperate*): Your
Grace!

BOLLIGREW: Yes Lord Mayor?

Two huge MEN-AT-ARMS *close in on* LORD MAYOR.

Got somethin' to say?

LORD MAYOR: . . . No, my lord.

BOLLIGREW: Oh sorry. Thought you 'ad. Lord Mayor Your Grace, just recently appointed 'im a Magistrate. (*Rueful.*) Independent minded little beggar. But I like the people to take part in their own government.

DUKE: Most commendable. But, Oblong—?

BOLLIGREW: He's been goin' to seed pretty rapid since he landed I'm afraid. If it isn't wine-gums it's brandy-snaps. And it takes 'im very nasty.

DUKE: Smoothe! Do you hear this?

SMOOTHE: Yes Your Grace. As Your Grace may remember, I always had my reservations about Oblong.

DUKE: You did, yes, you did.

BOLLIGREW: A good man in 'is day, I believe?

DUKE: The best I ever had!

BOLLINGREW: (*nodding*): My friend Doctor Innocent 'ere – 'e's a very penetratin' observer of the 'uman scene - he tells me when you're like that, you know, keepin' yourself on a very tight rein, then you're likely to go downhill very rapid if once you *let yourself go.*

Looks off as he says this phrase. Cheerful.

And 'ere 'e is! (*Expression changes.*) Oh dear oh dear . . .

Enter OBLONG, *swaggering, carrying packet of sweets. All, flinch, amazed.*

OBLONG: So! You finally got here! You backsliding old gormandizer.

Consternation among all.

BOLLIGREW: 'E's on the wine-gums again.

MAGPIE (*amazed*): Ark!

OBLONG: Mike Magpie. How you doin', Mike? The only
creature on these Islands I would care to call my friend.

Takes sweet from the packet.

BOLLIGREW: The bird is a notorious thief, Your Grace.

Exclamation from SMOOTHE.

OBLONG: Mike, meet Smoothley-Smoothe. Slipper
Smoothe we used to call him. Interesting man. Give you a
sound opinion on anything under the sun and sell you his
mother for threepence.

Swaggers on to DUKE.

Well, we've put it on a bit haven't we? (*Chuckles, prodding*
DUKE's *stomach.*) How many chocolate eclairs have gone
into that, I wonder? Whoops-a-daisy!

The DUKE *is rocking, pop-eyed on his heels as* OBLONG
prods. Total consternation among all.

SMOOTHE: But this is scandalous! (*Turns.*) The National
Anthem! Play the National Anthem!

'Colonel Bogey' again. All rigidly to attention, eyes popping as
OBLONG *breaks gradually into a disgraceful can-can, presenting*
posterier to DUKE, *etc. Anthem stops,* OBLONG, *very excited,*
breathless.

OBLONG: Ha!

Snaps his fingers at DUKE. *Gathers himself. Daring.*

Knickers!

All clap hands over ears. OBLONG *laughs wildly. Exit*
OBLONG. *All babble.* DUKE *falls fainting into arms of*
SMOOTHE.

SMOOTHE: His Grace! His Grace is Unwell!

BOLLIGREW: Clear the field! Clear the field!

Exit PEASANTS *driven by* MEN-AT-ARMS. MAGPIE *and*
OBIDIAH, *'hide', behind Church.* SMOOTHE *has lowered*

DUKE *to ground.* MOLOCH *waving ginger beer bottle under* DUKE's *nose.*

MOLOCH: His Grace revives.

DUKE (*weakly*): Has he gone?

SMOOTHE: Yes, Your Grace.

DUKE (*seizing* BOLLIGREW's *wrist*): Oh, Bolligrew, this is the ruin of a noble spirit. Oblong! There never was one like him with a dragon!

BOLLIGREW: Alas, those days 'ave gone.

MOLOCH: Gone indeed. Oblong and our Dragon are on very friendly terms.

DUKE: Friendly—! Smoothe! Can I credit this?

SMOOTHE: It's my experience Your Grace that when a man fails in respect, then we may look to him to fail in anything.

DUKE: That's very sound, Smoothe. (*Scrambles up.*) And (*feeling his paunch*) failed in his respect he most emphatically has! But . . . *Oblong*?

BOLLIGREW: Goes over every afternoon to Dragon's den Your Grace. See it for yourself if you wish.

DUKE: The Dragon's den? What for?

MOLOCH: A purely social call so far as one can see.

BOLLIGREW: I sometimes wonder if 'e 'asn't some arrangement with the brute.

MOLOCH: Oh no.

BOLLIGREW: What other explanation is there?

BLACKHEART: Always leaves 'is sword outside.

MOLOCH: That's true, that's true.

DUKE: Gentlemen! You can *show* me this?

BOLLIGREW: This very afternoon Your Grace. I thought we'd 'ave a bite of lunch first: couple of roast oxen, three or four stuffed peacocks, nothin' elaborate.

DUKE: Chestnut stuffing?

BOLLIGREW: Yes, Your Grace.

DUKE: Then, gentlemen, to lunch and after that— Oh Oblong! Oblong! – To the dragon's den!

Exit DUKE, *followed by* SMOOTHE, BLACKHEART, BOLLIGREW. MOLOCH *cautiously watches them away, turns suddenly.*

MOLOCH: Now Mazeppa, as you see, we approach the climax.

MAZEPPA: Yes, Master.

MOLOCH: I'd be inclined to take a boat at once—

MAZEPPA: Master?

MOLOCH: But I haven't yet secured my fee from Bolligrew. Now listen carefully, my dear; go straight down to the harbour, hire a boat, and have it standing by. It's always possible that something may miscarry.

MAZEPPA: Yes, Master.

MOLOCH: Wait here. I'll bring our bags. (*Going.*) I packed them this morning.

Exit MOLOCH, MAZEPPA *standing front stage, looking over audience in attitude of waiting,* MAGPIE, *and* OBIDIAH *emerge from behind Church.*

MAGPIE: What'd I tell you?

MAZEPPA: Witchcraft?

OBIDIAH: Witchcraft.

MAZEPPA *turns.* OBIDIAH *hides again.* MAZEPPA *and* MAGPIE *confront one another.* MAGPIE *has one hand behind back.*

MAGPIE: Awk!

MAZEPPA: Awk.

MAGPIE: You're not from these parts, are you?

MAZEPPA: Me? From the Islands? (*Loftily.*) I'm from Oxford.

MAGPIE: Go on? You attached to the University, then?

MAZEPPA: Rather depends what you mean. I am personal assistant to Dr Moloch.

MAGPIE (*admiring*): Moloch the Magician? You must 'ave quite a head-piece on you.

MAZEPPA: I was chosen from a large number of applicants. Yes, I keep our Journal.

MAGPIE: Journal?

MAZEPPA: Journal, yes. A record of all our spells. I often think I could do better without Moloch than Moloch could without me.

MAGPIE: You keep a record of all your spells?

MAZEPPA: Yes.

MAGPIE: You keep it up to date, do you?

MAZEPPA: Oh, yes. Quite up to date.

MAGPIE: Is that Moloch coming now?

Looking off. MAZEPPA *looks to see.* MAGPIE *produces monstrous club from behind back, and deals* MAZEPPA *a great blow.*

MAZEPPA: Awk!

Falls into MAGPIE's *arms.* OBIDIAH *emerges from Church.*

OBIDIAH: Eh, Mike, whatever are you doing—?

MAGPIE: No time now – help!

They drag MAZEPPA *behind Church, just in time for* MAGPIE *to take up* MAZEPPA's *stance as* MOLOCH *enters.*

MOLOCH: There, my dear. That one has my clothes.

MAGPIE *takes case.*

This one our equipment.

MAGPIE *takes it, almost drops it from its weight.*

Careful!

MAGPIE: Blimey!

MOLOCH: Mazeppa, do you feel quite well?

MAGPIE: Dandy! Er – yes, Master.

MOLOCH: Mazeppa, you're not going to have one of your nervous attacks, I hope?

MAGPIE: Awk. Er – no, Master.

MOLOCH: Then off to the Harbour to find a boat. Myself I'm going to get my fee from Bolligrew. At lunch I hope – if not – the Dragon's den.

Exit MOLOCH. OBIDIAH *emerges.* MAGPIE *rummaging in case. Produces heavy ledger.*

OBIDIAH: My word – bit of quick thinkin' that was.

MAGPIE: What's this? (*The ledger.*)

OBIDIAH: Spells K to Z.

MAGPIE: This?

OBIDIAH: Spells A to K.

MAGPIE: Then this must be the Journal!

OBIDIAH: Right! (*Opens it.*) Here it is! 'Sunday. Performed Spell Grimbleboots. Client: Bolligrew. Victim: Oblong. Purpose: Deliver same to Dragon . . .' The old devil . . .!

MAGPIE: Look up Grimbleboots!

OBIDIAH: What for?

MAGPIE: It'll give the antidote!

OBIDIAH: The antidote! (*Flipping pages.*) 'Gattlefyg, Golli- pog, Grimbleboots!' . . . 'Ingredients, Method, Application, Antidote!' . . . (*A pause.*) 'No antidote exists for this spell . . .' (*He sits.*) Baron's done some evil in 'is day. But this beats all. (*Silence.*) Pity we can't put 'im under a spell . . .

MAGPIE: We can! Grimbleboots! If Grimbleboots gave Baron power over Oblong, Grimbleboots will give us power over Baron.

OBIDIAH: Stands to reason that does! Mike Magpie – it's you that should've been to that there University.

MAGPIE: Ha ha! Ingredients! What are the ingredients?

   OBIDIAH *reads while* MAGPIE *checks tins and bottles.*

OBIDIAH: Snakes' feet.

MAGPIE: Snakes' feet.

OBIDIAH: Baking powder.

MAGPIE: Baking powder.

OBIDIAH: Fish feathers.

MAGPIE: Fish feathers.

OBIDIAH: Table salt.

MAGPIE: No table salt.

OBIDIAH: Got that at 'ome.

MAGPIE: What else?

OBIDIAH: Er— (*Face falls.*) Oh deary, deary, me . . . A prized possession of the victims. Prized possession of Bolligrew's, phew.

MAGPIE: Ark!

OBIDIAH: What?

MAGPIE: You won't tell Obby? (*Backing towards nest.*) It was twinklin' you see. 'E left it on 'is dressin' table and the sun was shining, and the window was open and it twinkled, so . . . (*He dangles the huge gold watch.*) D'you think it'll do?

OBIDIAH: Do? Baron'll go ravin' mad when 'e misses that! That's 'is presentation piece! Well I never thought I'd live to thank a thievish Magpie! Right. Down to my cottage for the table salt. We'll work the spell and then— (*Pause. They look at one another*) the Dragon's den.

   Lights dim; backcloth descends as before. Enter MOLOCH *and* BOLLIGREW, *hastily.*

BOLLIGREW: Well. (*Turning to* MOLOCH.) If those are the table manners of a Duke, commend me to the nearest cormorant. Never 'ave I seen a man put back stuffed peacock the way 'e can.

MOLOCH: Bolligrew, I'm in a hurry.

BOLLIGREW: Aye! Right.

Goes to den mouth.

Hello?

Eyes switch on. BOLLIGREW *flinches.*

Oh, there you are.

DRAGON: Here I am, where is Oblong?

BOLLIGREW: Be comin' any minute.

DRAGON: And you want me to eat him.

BOLLIGREW: Well that's easy enough isn't it?

DRAGON: It is, Bolligrew, yes. That's what makes me, just a little, wonder . . .

BOLLIGREW: Oh you'll be doin' me a good turn old man, don't you worry— All set then?

DRAGON: All set, Bolligrew. (*Eyes switched off.*)

BOLLIGREW (*to* MOLOCH): Well. I'll go and bring up the Duke. Sorry you 'ave to go . . . (*Going.*)

MOLOCH: My fee. Sixty-five guineas.

BOLLIGREW (*piteous*): Moloch – I'm a ruined man!

MOLOCH: Rubbish.

BOLLIGREW (*pulls bag from pocket, can't part with it*): Knock off the shillings.

MOLOCH: No.

BOLLIGREW (*enraged*): 'Ere you are then. (*Thrusts it at him.*) And bad luck to yer! (*Exits.*)

MOLOCH: Good-bye.

He too is going, but pauses. Weighs money bag thoughtfully.

Opens it. Takes out coin. Unwraps gilt foil. Puts coin in mouth, eats it carefully.

I see . . . Chocolate money . . . Well Bolligrew, this time, you've overreached yourself!

Goes to den mouth.

Dragon!

Eyes switch on.

DRAGON: Yes, Moloch?

MOLOCH: I have just found out that you are the object of a conspiracy!

DRAGON: You amaze me, Moloch. Go on.

MOLOCH: Bolligrew has given Oblong mortified apples.

DRAGON: Oh yes?

MOLOCH: Yes. I assume he got them from the mainland.

DRAGON: *Must* have done, mustn't he? Any more.

MOLOCH: I'm afraid so. When you have eaten Oblong and have fallen dead.

DRAGON: Yes?

MOLOCH: Then Bolligrew and Blackheart with some show of gallantry will come in there and cut the tail off your corpse.

DRAGON: Really. Now why would they do a thing like that?

MOLOCH: The Duke is here.

DRAGON: Understand. Ingenious scheme, Moloch.

MOLOCH: It has a certain squalid cunning I suppose. Myself I will not be a party to it. In your place I should simply claw Oblong to death, and eat the gallant dragon slayers.

DRAGON: Well of course.

MOLOCH: Oh – Bolligrew is bringing up the Duke. I must go.

DRAGON: Moloch.

MOLOCH: Yes.

DRAGON: Very grateful for the information.

MOLOCH: Not at all.

DRAGON: No, no, Moloch. Information must be paid for.

MOLOCH: Oh...(*Hesitating.*) Perhaps you'll send me a cheque.

DRAGON: Cash, Moloch. (*Noise of coins on Speaker.*) Come and get it.

MOLOCH (*licking lips, fascinated but frightened, hovers at mouth of den*): Well I, er—

DRAGON: Let's see; these seem to be ten guinea pieces. One (*clink*) two (*clink*) three (*clink*) – come in Doctor, come in—
  MOLOCH *helplessly drawn into den, disappears from sight.*
  His voice too comes on Speaker:
  four (*clink*), five (*clink*)—

MOLOCH: It's very dark in here . . .

DRAGON: Can you manage? I'm up here. Six (*clink*), seven (*clink*)—
  On Speaker, a clatter and a little gasp from MOLOCH.
  Mind the bones. That's it. Eight (*clink*), nine (*clink*) – and—
  Roar from DRAGON; *shriek from* MOLOCH.

MOLOCH: Put me down! Put me down!

DRAGON: Moloch, I don't believe that *Bolligrew* thought up that little scheme.

MOLOCH: Help!

DRAGON: No. I think *you* did.

MOLOCH: Help!

DRAGON: Anyway, I'm hungry.

MOLOCH: Dragon – consider your stomach! I am the Regius Professor of Wickedness at—
  A shriek, cut short. Silence. Dreadful champing noise. Then:

DRAGON: Youugh . . .! Disgusting.
  Enter DUKE, SMOOTHE, BOLLIGREW, BLACKHEART, MEN-AT-ARMS, PEASANTS, LORD MAYOR.

BOLLIGREW: Shan't 'ave long to wait Your Grace. Oblong's always 'ere 'bout tea-time. Well Sir Percy – ever seen a den as big as that?

SMOOTHE: It is very big . . .

BOLLIGREW (*to* DUKE): You see why, up till now, no one's cared to tackle 'im.

DUKE: Up till now?

BOLLIGREW: Yes, I think today may be the day. Blackheart's fair spoiling for it.

BLACKHEART: Just say the word, Bolligrew, an' I'll be in there an' 'ave 'is tail off in a jiffy.

BOLLIGREW: Courage of a lion Your Grace.

Indignant roar from DRAGON. *All flinch. Then* BLACK-HEART *shakes fist and roars back.*

Oh yes, he's workin' up to it. Today's the day all right.

DUKE: You mustn't let him Bolligrew! That's not a one-man Dragon.

BOLLIGREW: One-man? Oh – I shall go in with 'im, naturally.

DUKE: Bolligrew!

BOLLIGREW: Matter of noblesse oblige, Your Grace. Er, if anything goes wrong, you'll not forget the poor and needy of these islands, will you?

DUKE (*moved*): Good Heavens Bolligrew. I'm overwhelmed. And all this while, Smoothe, Oblong – our official representative, is on familiar terms with the brute!

SMOOTHE (*dry*): Yes Your Grace. I can hardly believe it.

BOLLIGREW (*pointing*): You'll believe your own eyes I hope? *All look off.*

DUKE: It is. It's Oblong. Good Heavens – he's *whistling*! *Enter behind them* MAGPIE *and* OBIDIAH *who bears prominently watch.*

OBIDIAH: Baron Bolligrew!

At his tone, all turn.

BOLLIGREW: Don't bother me n— 'Ere! That's me presentation piece! (*Crosses; takes it.*) Where d'you get it?

MAGPIE: Ark ..

BOLLIGREW (*putting it on*): Oh you was it?

Whistling – 'Sir Eglamore' – approaches. All turn again, and as whistling gets louder, shuffle back to prepare for OBLONG'*s entrance. But:*

OBIDIAH: Baron, cartwheel!

BOLLIGREW *cartwheels. All turn to him.*

MAGPIE: Another!

OBIDIAH: Another!

MAGPIE: Twirligig!

BOLLIGREW *handsprings, crashes in sitting position, astounded.*

DUKE: Bolligrew—?!

All spin again as enter OBLONG, *whistling. Makes brisk semicircle. Sticks sword in stage frontstage. Pleasantly.*

OBLONG: Bolligrew. Smoothe, People.

And walks briskly towards den, drawing sweets from belt as he goes.

Have a wine-gum, Tum-tum?

DUKE: Certainly not!

OBLONG: Suit yourself.

Disappears into den.

BOLLIGREW: See! Just as I said!

OBIDIAH: Baron, call him back.

BOLLIGREW: Come back!

DUKE: Good Lord!

OBLONG *reappears.*

OBLONG (*pleasantly*): Yes?

DUKE: Smoothe – Smoothe – what's going on?

OBIDIAH: Your Grace. The Baron 'as Sir Oblong in 'is power. And I 'ave Baron in mine. Baron, tell 'im to remove 'is prized possession.

BOLLIGREW: Remove your prized possession.

OBLONG (*plucks mantle from back. Comes to himself*): Good heavens – Your Grace? Good Heavens – the Dragon's den – my sword—! What's happening here? (*Finds sweet packet in belt, looks at it, realizes what it is and throws it from him with horrified exclamation.*)

DUKE: Oblong is himself again. Old friend. I fear you have been foully practised on.

OBIDIAH: Tell 'is Grace it is so.

BOLLIGREW: It is so.

DUKE: Oh infamous!

OBIDIAH: And tell His Grace that you, not Sir Oblong had an agreement with the Dragon.

BOLLIGREW: I, not Sir Oblong, had an agreement with the Dragon.

LORD MAYOR: And have had this many a year—!

BOLLIGREW: And have had this – you shurrup!

OBIDIAH: And tell His Grace you did it with the aid of Dr Moloch, calling himself Innocent.

BOLLIGREW: Did it with the aid of Dr Moloch, calling 'imself Innocent, yes.

DUKE (*amazed by his comfortably obedient tone*): And you confess this freely?

BOLLIGREW: Do I blazes confess it freely! This man 'ere's bewitched me somehow – 'Ere...!

Fumbles to unfasten watch.

OBIDIAH: Baron. Hands off!

BOLLIGREW's *hands fly out at arm's length.*

BOLLIGREW: See! See? (*Turns for all to see him.*) An' if I'm not greatly mistook, the 'ole of this is 'ighly illegal!

OBLONG: That's perfectly true. Evidence obtained by witchcraft is no evidence whatever – and rightly so. Obidiah I am deeply displeased. Tell the Baron to remove his watch.

OBIDIAH   (*together, overlapping*): But Sir—
MAGPIE   Don't be daft—
                                          Eh, Obby—

OBLONG: Immediately, Obidiah.

OBIDIAH: Then Baron, take it off.

He does.

DUKE: Now Baron, repeat your story.

BOLLIGREW: I will do no such thing! Pack of lies from start to finish!

SMOOTHE: Oblong my dear man, you've destroyed your own case.

OBLONG (*quietly*): I can't help that Smoothe. I cannot countenance the use of witchcraft.

BOLLIGREW: Well I'm glad to see there's *one* honest man 'ere. Besides me! I tell you what Obby – we've been practised on you an' me! We'll 'ave the law on the lot of 'em. Uncover corruption in very 'igh places I dare say. Black'eart saw it. 'E'll be witness!

OBLONG: Bolligrew, you are a transparent rogue and I have nothing to say to you. I hope his Grace will send some worthy gentlemen to take my mission to a successful conclusion. (*He sounds bitterly sad.*)

DUKE: Oblong, what's this?

OBLONG: Your Grace I shall never forget how I misbehaved this morning.

DUKE: But you were made to.

OBLONG (*quite sharply*): I was not. I was made to let myself go. I let myself go and misbehaved myself. (*he turns sadly picks up the mantle*) I fell prey to Dr Moloch, by my vanity and pride.

DUKE: Oh Oblong, really, that's ridiculous.

OBLONG: Not at all. (*Walks towards sword, thoughtfully, lovingly, folding and stroking it.*) I used to say I was not worthy. If truth were told I thought I was too good. Here's my sword. Well, (*drapes mantle over sword*) I will never carry sword again.

BOLLIGREW: Eh, now look 'ere Obby—

Immediately all join in, following and vociferously begging, cajoling, urging him to stay, according to their different natures. 'Be a sport Obby, don't take it like that.' 'Don't leave us Sir Oblong, you're the first Knight Errant we ever 'ad and we don't wish for none better.' 'Oblong, my dear fellow, this is really very fine drawn stuff; I wish you'd reconsider.' 'Look man, every blessed person here is asking for you.' 'Ark! Obby! Don't go off to the mainland now and leave us 'ere to Bolligrew.' 'Come on Obby, 'place won't be the same without you.' 'Sir Oblong, please – you are a familiar and well-loved figure in the Islands.' 'Remember 'ow we built the Church sir – what's to become of that?'

OBLONG (*repeats, but drowned so that we can only see his firmly upheld hand, his head shaking in refusal*):

No, no, I thank you, but my mind is made up.

DRAGON: My patience is exhausted!

Instant silence. All turn.

I can hear human beans. I can smell human beans. And – I'm – HUNGRY . . .!

On Speaker, noise of approaching DRAGON, *eyes get larger.*

ALL: The Dragon! The Dragon is at large!

They scatter, leaving OBLONG *isolated. A moment's hesitation, snatches mantle, wraps it round his arm, pulls sword from stage and rushes into den.*

OBLONG: An Oblong! An Oblong!

DUKE (*pointing*): Bolligrew! Redeem yourself!

Noise of conflict on Speaker.

BOLLIGREW: By Jove—! Tally-ho!

Crams cartridges into shotgun and follows OBLONG.

DUKE: Smoothe – assist them! Smoothe!

SMOOTHE *follows rather reluctantly.*

DUKE: Men-at-Arms!

They cheer and follow.

DUKE: Poor and needy!

They cheer and follow. Only BLACKHEART *left. Indignant, rhetorical:*

Squire Blackheart! Are you a gentleman or are you not?

BLACKHEART: No, I blazin' well am not!

Climax on Speaker to din of shouts, roars, clashing swords, banging of shotgun. Sudden silence. Gush of smoke. Then BOLLIGREW *and* OBLONG *emerge with huge black tail, followed by others all smoke blackened.*

DUKE: Oblong! Peerless Knight! You have surpassed yourself.

OBLONG: No no Your Grace. The principle credit belongs to the Baron.

DUKE: The Baron?

BOLLIGREW (*shaking his shotgun, beaming excited*): Got 'im with both barrels. A left and a right! Pow! Pow! Didn't I, Obby?

OBLONG: He did. The beast was on the wing too. Beautiful shots, Baron!

BOLLIGREW: By Jove, that's what I call sport! You can keep yer pheasants. Eh – these Dragons – can you breed 'em, artificial?

OBLONG: I never heard of it. But there are lots of wild ones.

BOLLIGREW: Where?

OBLONG: Up north. Dragons, Goblins, Lord knows what. Very good sport up north I believe.

BOLLIGREW: Black'eart, get ready to pack.

BLACKHEART: Now look 'ere, Bolligrew—

BOLLIGREW: You'll love it, Black'eart! (*Aiming gun at imaginary dragon.*) Pow! pow! Eh – what's the season?

OBLONG: All the year round.

BOLLIGREW: 'Ear that Black'eart – no closed Season. Well you needn't expect to see me back 'ere for some time, if at all.
Stir of delight among all.

BOLLIGREW: No, no, I shall be missed, I know that, but me mind's made up.
Enter STORYTELLER. *Rhymes commence.*

STORYTELLER: Then who will rule your people when you've gone?

BOLLIGREW: Fat lot I care – pow! pow! – Anyone.

DUKE: That timorous gentleman over there?

LORD MAYOR (*quailing under* BOLLIGREW's *appraisal*): I thank Your Grace, but I'll stay Lord Mayor.

DUKE: The bare-footed fellow showed some resource.

OBIDIAH: I'll stick to my trade, sir – thanks of course.

STORYTELLER: Excuse me Your Grace but it is getting late.

BOLLIGREW (*puts arm round* OBLONG): There's a perfectly obvious candidate!

STORYTELLER: And I ask you to name him with one voice.

ALL: Oblong Fitz Oblong!

STORYTELLER: The people's choice – Sir I salute you in a world of smiles. First Baron Oblong of the Isles – and that of course concludes the play—

OBLONG: It certainly doesn't. I've something to say.

STORYTELLER *looks at him, struck by indignant tone.*

We've killed a Dragon, and mended a quarrel—

STORYTELLER: What of it—?

OBLONG: – What of it sir? The *moral*!

As OBLONG *steps forward.*

STORYTELLER: I beg your pardon. But please keep it short.

OBLONG: It's simply this: My dears, do-what-you-ought. When there's something you want, and you can't do without it. There are various ways of going about it—

MAGPIE *(righteous)*: And a very good way is to – do – what – you – *should.*

OBLONG: Exactly.

MAGPIE: But a bit of what you fancy, does yer good!

OBLONG: Michael!

MAGPIE: Awk!

Music.

CURTAIN